LUSAKA CONFIDENTIAL

CHARLES MWEWA

ISBN: 978-1-998788-95-8

CONTENTS

It is a love affair made in purgatory – between the son of the most notorious drug lord and founder of the Arrogance Cartel, the biggest outlaw organization Zambia had ever known, Mwanga Bwembya, nicknamed, the Boss Boy, and the sweetest brave soul daughter of the most powerful lady bishop Zambia had ever produced, Monde Mwendashi, nicknamed, the Holy Girl.

On the surface, it seemed like the battle of emotions, but down under, it had all the conditions to turn a once most peaceful Christian nation on earth into a labyrinth of a failed state.

There was only one hope, the *Plan*.

[1] BOSS BOY MEETS HOLY GIRL

The Kabulonga Integrated High School for Highfliers or KISS, was the nation's most prestigious secondary school, rivaled only by its sister school, Ibex Secondary School. Students from these two schools were consistently ranked highest in terms of mental agility, likelihood of being hired for top jobs in the country, and intelligence quotient. Merely being associated with its name was prestigious - boys and girls across Zambia would do anything to be accepted into the school.

But it was different for the rich, the powerful and children from the high-ranked political establishments. And it was not a secret in the nation that second only to achieving highest on one's Grade 12 examination, money and influence played a key role for one to feature on the enrollment register for KISS.

But for one student, the criteria did not fit his pedigree. He was neither exceptionally intelligent nor from a wealthy, politically influential or powerful family. In fact, no one even knew who his parents were, except for a few, and those few chose to remain silent to avoid lethal repercussions.

They called that student the Boss Boy. He went unchallenged. His word was law. He sat in class, listened to lectures, and even asked questions, but he neither wrote his assignments nor submitted any. Everything was done by an army of assistants and bodyguards they called the *Assistanzas*.

Then came a girl, moderately beautiful, of average height and intelligence. But she carried an aura of invisibility, sacredness, and flawlessness. The first book she took out of her handbag when she sat at her desk was the Bible. The first book she packed in her handbag when class was over, was still the Bible. Her classmates nicknamed her the Holy Girl. Even the *Assistanzas* paid attention to her, and so did their boss.

***

"Why are those seats empty and they have been so for a long time?" Monde asked Gertrude.

There was a long pause. No one dared to say it; everyone pretended that they never heard what Monde Mwendashi had said.

"He's not yet in," whispered Gertrude to Monde, pretending to be picking up a pencil sharpener she had deliberately dropped.

"Who's he?" Monde asked, shouting loudly enough to catch Mr. Musonda, their class teacher's attention.

Before Gertrude could answer, Mr. Musonda interrupted.

"Some of you just enjoy being noisy. No noise, some of you are revising calculus for the mid-exam."

The way everyone gestured after Mr. Musonda's remarks left Monde with the impression that the class did not take him seriously, or that he was being hypocritical.

Then there was the sound of a whistle right outside the door. Monde wondered if she had made a mistake by moving from Ibex Secondary School to KISS. It was so audible that one might think it was the sound of a soccer match.

He was being escorted by seven bodyguards. There were three in front and four at his back. When he entered, everyone including Mr. Musonda acted as if they had not seen him.

Monde did not know what was happening. She was the only one who lifted up her head.

Then, as if he were being sliced into pieces, her sharp gaze met his. It shattered his sense of pride into fragments of tenderness. He had never seen such graceful eyes before.

Who is she?' It was more a rhetorical question than an inquiry.

Khalebb, his lead bodyguard had already jumped out to try and get Monde. He was about to strike her with his right fist when a familiar face appeared right before he unleashed a burst.

It was him. It was Mwanga, whom everyone at KISS called Boss Boy.

"Young master, I am so sorry I didn't…" Khalebb was struggling for words, when Boss Boy whispered to him authoritatively, "Not this one!"

***

"We…were…waiting for you, Mr. Mwanga," apologized Mr. Musonda to

Boss Boy.

As the Boss Boy was finishing to nod with his hand, Monde shot up like a rocket and addressed Mr. Musonda.

"I am so confused, sir, but aren't you the teacher here, but why are you apologizing to tha-t...tha-t...boy?"

Before the teacher could even speak, the seven bodyguards stood up and they gestured to Boss Boy that they should "teach the new girl a lesson."

"No one does anything to her, and that includes you, Mr. Musonda," Boss Boy commanded.

In unison as if they were being choreographed, the entire class, including the teacher said, "Yes."

Thumping herself hard in her seat, which was just three desks away from Boss Boy's, she let out her frustration and said, "This is unbelievable!"

Everyone heard her.

With a gesture of concern, Mr. Musonda signaled to Khalebb to meet him in his office. When they met that morning, Mr. Musonda did not know how to begin.

"To tell you the truth, I am running out of ideas how to protect the identity of the Patron…"

"Oh, sorry for interrupting you…for us in the *Assistanzas*, it's a nightmare, sir. We are firing on all fours, just to make sure that no one finds out that his family, in fact, *he* owns the school…let alone that he's the kingpin's son…"

"At least, Khalebb, ask the Patron to tread lightly with that new girl, Monde, she's also a force of nature…"

"Sir…we're trying. She's…but there are signs, sir, that Boss is falling in love with her…"

"Oh, my gash, isn't it so?"

"It can be collaborated by my friends…"

"No, Khalebb, don't bring trouble to yourselves, I will find a way to manage the class."

***

Agonizing in his empty room, empty bed, Boss Boy touched himself offhandedly. And spoke to himself, "I must have her. I must."

His bodyguard outside the door heard something but wasn't sure. "The last guard was exterminated just because he forgot to change a sheet of tissue paper. I must confirm if BB is actually calling me."

"Did you call me or say something, sir?"

"No. Or yes. Can you bring that girl to me, like now?"

"Which girl, sir?"

Boss Boy did not say anything. The

silence was enough for Clement Kopala to infer that the only girl to have taken his boss' interest was Monde.

"Sure, boss. Right away!"

Clement clothed himself in a toga, leather gloves and a helmet. He jumped ninja like on the utility motorcycle and off he went to Gertrude's house.

When he arrived at house number 4 Ikolongo Road, off Bwanankubwa Vet Clinic, he honked so loud that the entire neighborhood heard.

She walked out wrapped in a greenish brown chitenge gown. Timidly, she asked, "Can I help you, Clement?"

Gertrude had no problem recognizing Clement. Of all the seven bodyguards, Clement was the most recent to be hired, and the only one hired directly from the same class Boss Boy attended. Clement doubled both as student attaché and bodyguard. An ultra-smart boy? Clement also performed all the homework assignments for Boss Boy.

"I saw you with Monde in class. Do you have her address or know who does?" Clement asked.

"Yes, but…" Gertrude hesitated.

Clement let his left arm drop, simultaneously revealing a small black knife.

"I know. I know, Clement. It's just that she lives at the Grand!"

"What? You mean…"

"Yes."

"Bishop's…"

"Yes…in fact, her only daughter."

All that Gertrude saw was dust left behind. The tough and smart boy had left just as soon as he heard Bishop's. He said no word.

"*This* is going to be interesting," Gertrude sighed, and banged her door shut with a very long smile.

***

"Is she in the living room, Clement, it's the first time you've been this efficient, did she give you trouble?" Boss Boy asked.

"No... no, Boss, it's not like that."

"What's it, she was expecting me, she loves me, right?"

There was uncharacteristically a very long pause even leaving an awkward moment. Boss Boy was getting impatient. He was already mixing various combinations of perfumes with his home assistant, Maureen.

"Does this befit a princess, Mo?"

"Sure, Boss. By the way, Boss, who's this lucky girl who seems to have conquered your heart?"

There was another pause. Then he spoke.

"I have never seen such graceful eyes drawn on the canvas of elegance and beauty. My eyes almost went blind, my heart almost stopped."

"Wow, Boss. That must have been something."

"And you know something, she seemed like my late mother. I couldn't let anybody lay a hand on her."

"But…"

"But what, Mo?"

"Nothing, Boss."

Just then Clement interrupted.

"Boss, actually, I didn't come with her."

Boss Boy jumped off the dresser and roared.

"What you… do you have a death wish?"

"No, Boss."

"But what?"

"She's Bishop's daughter, sir."

"Wha…what did you say?"

"Monde, sir, is Bishop Mwendashi's only daughter, I have just learned."

Boss Boy sunk into his chair like a blunt. Ten minutes passed and no one said a word.

"OMG, are you sure?"

"Yes," answered Clement.

***

It was Monday.

And that meant a resting day for Zambia's grandest clergywoman. In fact, it was only seventeen years ago when she was referred to by the *Times of Zambia* as "grandest" bishop after the Grand Cathedral was erected.

The project to build the cathedral had begun 30 years prior when Beatrice Mwendashi was only a reverend. She assumed leadership of the former Presbyterian Temple after the untimely demise of its founder and reverend and founder, Paul George, the last of the colonial fraternities in the previously British colonial territories in Africa.

An eccentric moderately beauty, Beatrice had founded a charismatic movement within the central presbytery as they called all the units of the Presbyterian Synod of central Zambia.

She had been sent abroad to Texas to study business administration at the University of Houston (UofH). She was barely 17. And rumors have it that it was while she was at UofH that she was invited by a roommate to attend a Pentecost Church service. There, she got baptized in the Spirit with the evidence of speaking in tongues.

When she returned home, she was nicknamed "Electricity Sister," because when she prayed, the room was electrified as they said it in ecclesiastical parlance.

As years passed, she successively rose in rank from Charisma Church movement leader to deacon and to associate reverend, and when Rev George died, to the head of the Chilonganino Presbyterian Church.

She quickly transformed the traditionally mainstream church into a vibrant tongue speaking, tithe gathering and demon casting church. After spending 30 days on the South Korean Yoido Church mountain of prayer sabbatical, she returned to Zambia and reformed the Chilonganino Church into a megachurch. The church mainly grew through a tripartite vision of church cell groups, tithe collection and deliverance services. As people were saved, they were simultaneously being schooled into the intricacy of financial and business enterprises. Within few years, the once small ministry under Rev. George, had become the envy not only of Zambia, but of the rest of Africa.

Then the announcement.

It came from nowhere. She was preaching on a church growth series from the Book of Nehemiah when in the middle of the lecture she stopped and said, "God told me that this place is too small for us, we must build for him a grand cathedral."

And that's how the idea of the Grand Cathedral was born.

The mobilization to build the cathedral was dubbed a local miracle by the international press and media. *Fox News* once reported:

> When you land at an innocuously looking Kenneth Kaunda International Airport, and a rusted dusty taxi takes you into the inner city.
> "The inner city consisted of the mostly poverty-stricken meandering mixture of run-down shanty compounds and elegant modern architectural gated streets, you come to

what should be a paradise on earth. It comes out of nothing, a golf course, a small airstrip, a modern shopping plaza and its own gas station, all meant for one lady. Then you make a corner, and boom, a mammoth of a building. Silhouetted by palm trees and elegant mahogany shrubs, you enter in what can only be described as Solomon's twenty-first century temple. And then you are told that all that you saw were sacrificial given by the extremely poor people and their poor surroundings, and you fail to understand how.

However, there were many people who doubted that the money to build the cathedral came squarely from the poor.

And that list of people was growing.

"Monde, the pilot has been waiting, come on my queen, let us go," a soft but stern prompt issued from the Grand Cathedral's tycoon.

"Oh, Mother, I thought that we'll be doing our shopping around the plaza here?"

"No, my queen, there is a special type of butter spread the kitchen told me can only be found in Cape Town, South Africa. We're headed there, will be back soon. Besides…"

"Besides what?"

"You didn't tell me what happened at your new school?"

"Mother!"

The mother and her only daughter boarded the bishop's plane and set off to South Africa for shopping.

***

"Kindly fasten your seat belts, Your Grace, and Madam Monde. We're taxing for takeoff. Thanks," Mike 'Polopela' Mwansa, advised.

"Sure," Monde answered.

Although she used to fly almost every day, Bishop Beatrice Mwendashi had not fully accustomed herself to it. There was momentary silence until the pilot navigated the small four-seater Boeing aircraft to stability at the altitude of about three thousand meters above the ground.

After about seven minutes later, Polopela announced again, "It's safe to take off your belts, ma'ams."

She turned slightly forward and said, "Now, I want to hear your escape at your new school, my queen."

Monde, who was sitting in front of her mother simply nodded and her mother saw it.

As per protocol, Bishop Mwendashi always sat at the back. When flying, her pilot also served as her bodyguard to reduce costs, as she informed the church board. However, when travelling on commercial flights abroad, she took at least two bodyguards with her. These bodyguards were paid for by the Ministry of Foreign Affairs of Zambia at the instigation of President Zeibous, whom she had helped rise to power. In addition, her travels abroad were considered diplomatic missions, and she carried a Zambian diplomatic passport with her.

"I met a true bully, Mother."

"Say it again," Bishop Mwendashi had meant it as a rhetorical question. Very quickly a thought of fear passed furiously through her nerves. She had just facilitated the transfer from Ibex Collegiate High School to her present school because Monde complained about being swarmed by paparazzies and other students who wanted autographs from her.

At her new school, only her servant girl, Gertrude, and her bodyguard, Francis, who both pretended to be classmates, knew of her true identity. She was registered as Monde M. Malupenga to divert attention from her because of her mother's popularity in the country.

President Zeibous had called the principal of the new school and warned him, thus, "Don't let anyone know that she's the bishop's daughter, you understand?" And Mr. Mumbi Mushota had assured the president that as the principal he would do everything to keep the secret.

"They call him Boss Boy. He owns the classroom including the teacher. He enters with pomp and majesty, surrounded by a septet of retinue. Yesterday, he handed in an assignment written by his bodyguard, Mother!"

What, what are you trying to tell me, but President Zeibous does not have a boy, she thought.

"What did you say, Mother, I only heard the first…"

Just then, Polopela announced that they were taxing for landing in South Africa.

"Tighten your belts and put your seats in the upright positions. Thank you."

And in less than ten minutes, they touched down and landed safely and smoothly.

"We will continue our conversation later."

"Sure, Mother."

[2] THE HUNCH

“It pains,” she started thinking.

“This thought pains me so much, Lord, you must deliver me from this thorn,” the elegant Bishop prayed.

She remembered.

They were the most ambitious of the seventeen boys the colonial government had handpicked to be trained as spies for what would later become Zambia. They excelled in tactics and infiltration methods to the extent that they successfully served the last British governor of Rhodesia, preventing his assassination. In return, the British government and the incoming Zambian government had made a pact to honor the two boys and their descendants with government posts in perpetuity.

Zeibous Mukangalume (nicknamed "Muka") and Mumba Makayi Milando Bwembya (nicknamed, the "General," or "Mila" as Beatrice called him) were like conjoined twins. They thought alike and had been allies in all their operations under the supervision of the "Mother."

She was ruthless as she was deliberate. She was the invisible matriarch of the first Zambian freedom fighters. But she had one daughter.

Beatrice was born under very unusual circumstances. She was born in the bush during the Rhodesian-Nyasaland War, and no one knew who her father was - she didn't know him either. As a result, she grew up extremely overprotected.

Her mother was the Mother.

But Beatrice hated thuggery and the life of patronage. She once had a heated argument with her mother, the Mother.

"You want me to abort this child, but I won't, Mother."

"You must. That boy you love is trouble. I trained him but he's not a team player. He's got canning tendencies. Marry Zeibous instead."

"But Mumba Makayi Milando Bwembya is my child's father, and not Zeibous."

"I know, Beatrice, but…."

"But what, no, Mother. Over my dead body."

"No, Beatrice. You're mistaken, it's over mine!"

The mother and her daughter argued over the right choice for Beatrice. One option was Mumba Makayi Milando Bwembya, the man she loved and the apparent father of her unborn child.

Mumba Makayi Milando Bwembya was notorious and self-willed. The other option was Zeibous, a thinker and tactician, but he was aloof and an impassioned politician. She hated Zeibous.

"I didn't tell you before, darling, but my days are numbered. I am dying, I have cancer."

Beatrice hugged her mother and apologized. The duo cried in each other's arms. And at the end of the day, they had reconciled to Beatrice marrying Zeibous because, according to the Mother, "He's a responsible boy."

But Zeibous didn't know that Beatrice was pregnant. The pregnancy was not his; Beatrice was carrying Mumba Makayi Milando Bwembya's child.

Beatrice had to tell Mumba Makayi Milando Bwembya that their private affair was over. She knew that he would not take it well, both because of his temper and the love he had for her. So, when she told her Mother about her dilemma, her mother suggested that she should go with Zeibous.

"Zeibous, Mother. They're best friends!"

"So, what, remember my health, mhm."
Beatrice loved her mother; she was the only parent who raised her. The disclosure that her mother was terminally ill had taken the wind out of her sails. She felt pity for her dying mother.

"Alright, Mother," Beatrice gave in, reluctantly.

It was at noon in October. The sun had risen in the sky and an inviting breeze was blowing across the horizon. She was wearing a green skirt with a long brown blouse. On her head was a red wrapper with a brownish tiara. She carried a brown handbag in her left arm, while holding onto Zeibous' right biceps as they approached Mumba Makayi Milando Bwembya.

It was obvious that something was wrong.

"Before you say anything, let me explain," Beatrice started.

"I know. Mother told me that you'd be telling me something serious. And seeing you hand in …"

"Ssh," Beatrice interrupted.

Zeibous didn't say a word.

"Why, I knew you first," Mumba Makayi Milando Bwembya complained. Zeibous still said nothing.

"But I have made my choice."

"What choice, yours or Mother's?"

As the duo retreated hand in hand, it pained Mumba Makayi Milando Bwembya even the more. He kept quiet for a long time before he nodded and said to himself, "I know what I'll do."

***

It had been over six months since Mumba

Makayi Milando Bwembya and the couple had a confrontation, and nearly four months since the Mother succumbed to cancer. Beatrice was due to give birth. When she woke up that day, she was in a makeshift hospital.

"Calm down. He's Zambia's greatest physician. You'll soon and officially be a mother," said the unusually loving voice of the man she was so familiar with, echoing into an empty but clean thatched room.

It's Mumba Makayi Milando Bwembya, she thought.

Dr. Martin Phiri instructed the soon-to-be mother to relax and breathe. She felt neither pain nor pleasure. But there was all manner of machinery around her. She quickly learned that power was being generated by a generator outside the room when Dr. Phiri said to a man standing beside him.

"Make sure that the generator is running properly and that the epidural is working correctly."

"Sure, Doc.," the man had responded.

Within a span of two hours Beatrice had given birth to a bouncy baby boy. But she never got to see him or breastfeed him. Soon as labour was over and she had been restored to health, Beatrice was whisked away to the University Teaching Hospital (UTH) where she had been kidnapped.

No sooner had she gained consciousness than she discovered she was back at UTH, but not in her ward. She was in Dr. Phiri's office.

Beatrice knew that it was the same doctor who had delivered her baby when she saw his photo on the wall, but she feigned ignorance for the safety of her child.

Why can't I recognize that place? Beatrice contemplated.

She had been asked by the police if she could recall where she was delivered from and how she got there and back.

"As I have been saying, I didn't know. Soon as I was assisted by that man on that picture, I lost consciousness. When I regained my consciousness, I was here."

And when she was asked if she knew who the mastermind was, she again concealed the truth. She was afraid that if they knew that it was CXX, the baby would be in danger.

She said, "I never heard or saw the mastermind. Dr. Phiri left the room twice I think to receive instructions from someone but I never saw them."

When the interrogation ended that day, she argued within herself, "*I know it's Mumba Makayi Milando Bwembya.*"

She remembered Mumba Makayi Milando Bwembya having a conversation with Dr. Phiri just before the baby was born. When Mumba Makayi Milando Bwembya had asked the doctor to confirm if, indeed, that child who was about to be born was his, Dr. Phiri affirmed it with an emphatic, "Yes, General; I am 100%. DNA

31

results confirm it. It's 99.999% in favor of your parentage."

It is certainly him, his voice and title. Everyone addresses him as 'General,' she had thought.

The days that followed were very hard for Beatrice. She had started to resign herself to her fate. Police investigations into the baby's disappearance did not bear any fruit. Beatrice had informed the police that she gave birth to a live child. And since helping her to give birth, no one had seen or heard of Dr. Phiri and his family. They simply vanished. Everyone concluded that they had been kidnapped, but whether they consented to it or not, was unknown.

When days became weeks and weeks months, and then months became years, the investigation went cold. After three and a half years, Beatrice became pregnant again with Zeibous' child. She gave birth to a healthy baby girl whom she named Monde. However, her interest in men had been seriously damaged by the disappearance of her first-born baby. She called off her engagement to Zeibous under the arrangement that he would contribute to Monde's upkeep.

The agreement was witnessed by a notary and signed by both Beatrice and Zeibous. Beatrice kept the original copy.

***

At church, everyone knew that Monde had no father. When Beatrice went abroad to study, Monde remained with a relative until she returned after three years.

Monde had not been told who her father was until five years later when, out of nowhere, Beatrice told her.

"That man on TV is your biological father."

"But that's the president, Mother?"

"Yes, *he*'s the one."

Monde was more confused than furious. She then began to put two and two together. The government funded her education. The government offered her mother a personal plane. The government provided local security to her and her mother. And the government gave her money and a diplomatic passport.

Oh, my Gosh, everyone thinks that Mother has achieved all these in her own power, she thought.

Monde began to talk to her mother again after a weeklong of contemplative silence.

"Mother, I have a question for you."

"Sure, my queen."

"Why didn't you marry the president?"

"Oh, Darling, it's a long story. Probably, I will answer that one day when you begin to have children of your own."

"Okay, fine. But I have one more question, oops, two."

"Go ahead. I may answer if it's right."

"Does he, I mean, the president know that I am his daughter?"

"Of course, he does. But we have an arrangement."

"An arrangement? Does that mean not having a father-daughter relationship?"

"That's not fair," Monde was visibly upset.

Beatrice tried to comfort her daughter. But she struggled to find proper words. She knew that her daughter must know, but it wasn't easy to explain how things transpired. In addition, reality was too daunting a task to unveil plainly.

"But he cares for you and me ever since he became president, though…"

"Though what?" Monde pounced.

Beatrice wanted to say that she was instrumental in Zeibous' rising to power and, therefore, all that the government did to them was deserved, it was not easy to explain it.

"There are certain things that must not be explained, my queen."

"But you are the one …"

"…teaches honesty and integrity, I know. But even God has secrets he would reveal until at the right time!"

"So, are you still seeing him, I mean, are you having sex with him?"

"Oh, God, no. It's been strictly business. I have long passed from death to life by the grace of God."

Monde's misgivings about men only grew stronger. She had long wondered why she grew up not knowing her father and now she knew that her father had been around but not present.

Men are shit, forgive me Lord for using an unsavory language. But I can't stop to think why he shouldn't have claimed me publicly as his daughter! Monde thought.

However, two things had made Monde transition almost unscathed by the news. First, it was the love her mother had given her throughout her upbringing. She never thought she needed a father as long as mother was alive. And second, her mother had taught her and the congregations she pastored that God was the father of the fatherless. To Monde, that was enough. Although from time to time she wished that she had a brother or sister and a resident father, she would immediately dismiss it for the privileges she enjoyed which not so many people in the world could afford.

"I am blessed beyond measure," she once told her maidservant and confidante, Gertrude.

[3] THE PURSUIT

Mwanga Bwembya, popularly known as the Boss Boy, stretched himself from his bed. He had not slept a bit since he laid eyes upon Monde.

"She was as gorgeous as she was graceful," he said, matter- of -factly, as he entered the dining hall for his breakfast.

He remembered the first time he laid his eyes on her, at KISS.

She was beautiful, like a black diamond, with funneled broad lips canopied in darkish pink lipstick. Her bust, elevated by a strapless bra, her hips, of the elongated elevation, held firmly by slightly protruding buttocks, blunted only by a knee-high branching red dress, and a thong less selection of underwear. She had angel-like oval-shaped eyes, camouflaged by straight black eyebrows, in darkly glaring hazel stars. She walked majestic, in the framework of an endeared peacock. She sat down as she stood up, attentive to every detail, sharp like a razor but graceful like the fledgling neck of happy giraffe.

"Who was *she*, Master?" Melody Mbewe, the dutiful handmaiden asked, teasingly.

"Oh, my goodness, Melody, I…"

"I can tell, Master…"

"Tell what, Melody?"

"Don't be mad with me, Master. Since I started taking care of you when you were left under my care, I have never seen you this happy…"

"So, you concluded that I am…"

"…very much in love, Master!"

"I think you got me there. Now, what do we have here for breakfast?"

"Mhm…" hummed Melody.

"Oh, Melody, before I forget, and since you're the closest thing I have ever had for a mother, tell me, who was my mother?"

Melody agonized within. She had strict instructions not to tell Boss Boy anything about his mother. She remembered how she was hired to take care of Baby Mwanga in the first place.

Two men had invaded a midwifery wing of the Chilenje Midwifery Hospice (CMH) and abducted her in the middle of the night. She was only twenty-one years old. The first thing she saw when she entered the black tinted minivan was a cuddly baby swashed in a fluffy brown blanket. It was adorable as it was helplessly defenseless in the hands of rough looking man with a gun in one of his hands.

She was immediately handed over to the baby. Melody Mbewe had joined CMH after a personal tragedy. She had conceived after being raped in a brothel and, to her colleagues' amazement, she had opted to keep her baby.

Her friends decided to take her to CMH, which had a wing for unclaimed pregnancies where they used experimental delivery exercises for their students. Unfortunately, Melody's child died after birth, and she still had milk in her breasts.

Boss Boy's father, the ringleader of Zambia's first drug cartel, had threatened CMH's chief executive officer to provide a suitable student as a wet-nurse or he would kill his entire family. It so happened that Melody, who had just lost her child, had signed up to remain at CMH to learn midwifery.

That day she held the baby; she fell in love with him, and for the past nineteen years, she has raised him as her own child. Boss Boy had never called her "mother." From the beginning, Boss Boy's father had warned Melody to treat him as "your boss; he is your boss."

So, that morning, Melody remembered her obligation not to discuss intimate details of Boss Boy's parentage, brushed aside his question about his mother and sustained the flowery moment of the time.

"Young Master, you are blushing," Melody diverted.

"Me, never."

Boss Boy had been brought up to consider feminine qualities and attributes as weaknesses. Blushing was one of them. But instead of getting mad as he would in normal circumstances, that morning, Boss Boy was in high spirits, and he took it calmly.

Melody never answered the question not because she knew the answer herself, but because she had also been trying to figure it out. When she first began to care for him, she had heard rumors that the child's mother was the Boss' most beloved ex-girlfriend. She also heard that the mother's name was Beatrice, but nothing more was said after that.

That's all Melody knew.

That morning, every one of the twenty-seven workers in the 'Mansion' was amazed to see a side of Boss Boy they had never witnessed before. He was gentle, forgiving and appreciative.

"I want to see Master like this every day," Mirimba Gowani began.

"Me, too," Monica Ndelele, concurred.

"Girls, go back to work, no more gossip," ordered the head of Mansion protocol, Melody Mbewe.

They all went their own ways doing their respective chores.

***

But Mwanga was just beginning his plot to win Monde over at all costs. He lined up classmates, friends and paid recruits to spy on Monde and gather information about him. The entire week, he instructed his bodyguards to bring Monde breakfast and lunch and to keep an eye on her.

Monde did not accept any of his offers and gifts but that didn't discourage him.

"My lady, it will not offend to accept at least his offer of breakfast," Gertrude. advised

"No. Gertrude, you know boys, that's how they begin."

"But he's cool, and rich."

"So, what, Gertrude, I can claim the same."

"But…"

"But what, Gertrude, you're overthinking."

"I am sorry, ma'am, I just need to say it."

"Go ahead and say it."

"I told them that you are Bishop's daughter…"

"What?"

"I had to, I had no option, ma'am. They knew my hostel and they came every day. I felt pity for them and thought that they would be restrained if they knew that you were very important…"

"Even though, Gertrude, you know the reason why we came here, don't you?"

"I do, ma'am."

"Which is?"

"That you needed to be free from the disturbers."

"And then, what have you done?"

"If I may speak freely now, ma'am, please punish me after I speak…."

Monde glanced through her left eye and winked. Gertrude understood that it meant that she could say it without getting punished.

"He's not a paparazzi and he's cute. You will need a man…"

"Stop right there, Gertrude. He's…"

"A sinner, but, ma'am, people change. He can change, besides…"

"Besides what, is there anything I should know?"

"Yes, ma'am. He began coming to church."

"What?"

"I am telling the truth. He's been there twice now."

"I wonder what church can tolerate his pride."

"Ours, ma'am…"

Monde was visibly surprised, and she gave no apologies for interrupting Gertrude. But the dutiful handmaiden was not deterred, and she continued.

"He came without any bodyguards. He even answered the altar call. I mean, he lifted up his hand when Bishop gave the order. I think that he's Born Again. I'm sure of it."

Monde was dumbfounded, but she kept her cool at that moment. She didn't want Gertrude to notice that. Then she went into thinking.

"Is that why this week he took his own notes in class and even called Mr. Musonda 'sir'? That was the first time he'd done that since I joined the class. Gertrude may be right—he had no bodyguards in class this week. I mean, he had one, not seven."

The "Holy Girl," as people acquainted with her called her, was deep in thought when Gertrude interrupted her.

"My lady... my lady!"

She regained her temporary loss of consciousness and answered, "Oh, Gertrude, are you calling me?"

"Yes, ma'am, and..."

"You have more, Gertrude?"

"Yes, I do."

There were very few things on earth that not only excited the Holy Girl but also gave her enormous joy, and everyone around her knew it. It was the reason she had maintained her virginity despite having numerous opportunities to lose it.

She loved Jesus.

She prayed every day and encouraged all her workers to do the same. But she was not a typical Christian; she loved to party, too. She would sneak out from her room and take one of her bodyguards incognito to a nightclub far away from Lusaka. She preferred Chilanga to Kabwe because, as she told one of her bodyguards once, "I have escorted my mother for ministry in Kabwe several times, and many people there recognize me."

"Say it, Gertrude," she prompted.

"He's started reading the Bible."

There was total silence. None of them spoke a word for about five minutes. Then Monde challenged Gertrude.

"How do you know?"

"Because I read with him occasionally."

"Gertr…"

"It's not what you think, ma'am. His bodyguards pick me up from my hotel when you release me. They have my timetable. We read in his car, usually parked around the old Independence Stadium."

"Oh, is that the case? And how long has this been going on?"

"For six months now."

"You mean…"

"Yes, ma'am, in the past two months after we relocated from Ibex High."

"And how did it happen?" Monde asked, with steadfast resignation.

Then Gertrude recounted how Boss Boy had felt a connection the moment he laid eyes on Monde. He was smitten with something stronger than interest. According to Chisanshi, one of Boss Boy's trusted servants, he felt like he wanted to be with "this girl somehow."

"Then he launched an all-out investigation…"

"For what?" Monde interjected.

"To know more about you, ma'am."

Monde learned that Boss Boy had hired a brilliant private investigator from the Doxyorod Private Eye Professionals (DPEP), famously known across Zambia as "Deep."

"Deep's first task was to study…"

"Me," Monde said matter-of-factly.

"No, ma'am, it was to study me, actually," Gertrude explained.

Monde was disappointed, but she quickly realized that her nemesis was smarter.

"Why study you, Gertrude?" Monde wanted to know.

"I don't know, but I can guess," Gertrude said.

Monde did not say anything. She took chewing gum from her handbag, offered one to Gertrude, which she politely declined, and Monde continued to think.

Because by studying Gertrude first, they could discover my habits vicariously. That's like killing two birds with one stone, she thought.

The silence created a momentary friction gap. Gertrude winked guiltily, trying hard to break the awkward silence, but without success. Monde was fixated on squeezing every bit of sweetness out of the chewing gum. She wasn't even aware that she was chewing it.

Then, as if Gertrude had heard her thoughts, Monde vocalized, "*Genius, evil genius!*"

"What did you say, ma'am?" Gertrude asked.

Monde was relieved that Gertrude didn't hear her thoughts. And with resigned comportment she simply said, "Never mind."

***

It had been a long time coming. Monde M. Poloshi, as she was registered at KISS, had not spoken a word to Boss Boy except during class debates. And that only happened once, with Mr. Musonda's intervention.

During the only debate in which Monde

faced the Boss Boy, the topic of discussion was on reproductive freedom and the role of artificial insemination in guaranteeing a healthy society. Boss Boy shocked the class, including Monde, when he strongly suggested that natural selection can sustain life even without the physical presence of one parent.

Mr. Musonda was the only teacher who knew that Monde was the bishop's daughter and that she was secretly being promoted by the secret service. However, he did not know that Gertrude and another female student in his class were also part of the secret service, serving as bodyguards for Monde.

"We have all been oriented towards a strict father- mother relationship in the raising of a healthy family, but I grew up without a mother, in fact, I don't even know who my mother is," Boss Boy said.

Monde was internally shaken by that statement. She had thought that a strong family that secured the benefits of national pride was one built on strong moral values.

But in Boss Boy's statement, there was an implied truth that chance could be a good moral guide to a strong community.

I, too, was raised by a single loving and hard-working woman, she did just fine, Monde thought.

"Ms. Poloshi, your response to what Mr. B. just said," Mr. Musonda poked Monde who seemed absent minded. She had been taken aback by Boss Boy's statement. She was in deep thoughts. Then she composed herself and rejoined the conversation.

"Oh, me, I think I agree with Mr. B...whatever you call him," Monde said.

Everyone on Monde's team was surprised. They did not expect her to agree with Boss Boy. The entire class knew that Monde did not like Boss Boy. But they did also know that Boss Boy liked and tolerated Monde. They were not sure until that concession that Monde was capable of liking anyone, especially someone who was not even a Christian.

Then Monde made a gesture that made even Mr. Musonda laugh his lungs out.

"I think I agree with his reasoning, but not his lifestyle. And what does even Mr. 'B' mean?"

The class broke into laughter, the only time everyone truly laughed, and it was because Boss Boy was also laughing.

"He didn't take offence to that confrontation," one boy whispered to another boy.

"She's his match," a girl who was very far away in class from both Boss Boy and Monde, said to her neighbor. Her neighbor whispered back, "Be quiet, don't you know that Mr. B has ears and eyes all over.

"But he's laughing today," the first girl replied.

"Still, be quiet, things can change very quickly," the second girl advised.

"And why do they refer to him as Mr. B,

does 'B' mean his last name?" The first girl asked the second girl.

"You fool, it means 'Boss.' He's called Mr. Boss; don't you get it?" The second girl replied.

"No, you're both wrong," chipped in the third girl.

"If not Boss, what then does it stand for?" The second girl asked the third girl.

The third girl beckoned to both the first and second girls to get closer. Then she whispered in their ears.

"It's Bwembya. Like Bwembya the Mafia Boss."

The two girls expressed silent shock. They were dumbfounded and they jumped back and tucked themselves into their seats quietly.

The country's most powerful drug lord was a topic of discussion four years prior when he was publicly prosecuted. His name was a controversial aspect of establishing the identity of the criminal until in private session called a *voir dire* two witnesses were called to establish the drug lord's identity. And rumors had it that one of the witnesses was President Zeibous, and the other was a mysterious woman whose identity had never been revealed to the public.

The testimony of the duo established the identity of the country's most notorious drug trafficker and dealer as Milando Bwembya, famously known in the media as "Bwembya the Boss."

President Zeibous won his reelection two years ago partly because he used his testimony and promise to put the country's notorious drug cartel lord behind bars. The mysterious witness was also rewarded with secret service protection for the remainder of her life. The Kasongole Whistleblower Act, named after an MP from Kasongole Constituency in Central Province, extended secret service protection to the family and successors of the other mysterious witness.

"So, that's the reason why even Mr. Musonda fears him?" Whispered the first girl.

"Of course, yes," answered the third girl.

"Oh my gosh, Monde must be very daring," commented the second girl.

"I heard rumors," indicated the third girl.

"What rumors?" Asked the first girl, directing her question to the third girl.

"That she is…"

"We are going to take a short break.

Everyone, leave the classroom, except, of course, for Mr. B.," Mr. Musonda ordered.

Class was adjourned.

***

Everyone in Class B left except for Boss Boy, his three bodyguards, and Monde. Mr. Musonda lifted a small note and said, "I dismissed the class because of this note. Sir, you wanted to have a private chat with Ms. Poloshi."

"Yes..." and as he spoke, he was simultaneously signaling with his left hand to all the bodyguards to leave him and Monde alone.

As everyone was leaving the class, including Mr. Musonda, Monde also tried to stand up and leave. Boss Boy stood up quietly, ran toward Monde, went down on one knee, and pleaded, "I just want to talk. It will be brief, I promise."

Without saying a single word, Monde remained in her seat.

Without his bodyguards around, Mwanga struggled to adjust himself comfortably. He seemed more like a rat that was caught in a trap than the confident boy who commanded everyone around him.

"Mhm...hahaha," Monde laughed.

"What are you laughing about?" Mwanga teased, still struggling to find his composure.

"You," Monde replied, pointing her index finger in Mwanga's direction.

Boss Boy chewed on his upper lip and looked sideways. Then he slowly lifted himself up, majestically, and said, "Here I am."

Monde, seeing Mwanga up close for the first time, shuddered and almost fell off her chair. She was suddenly looking at a nineteen-year-old muscular man, five feet eight inches tall, wearing nothing but the most comforting smile she was familiar with but couldn't quite remember from whom.

"Peace," Mwanga said, as he volunteered to catch Monde who was internally shaking.

"I…a…m, mhm, al-right," Monde stammered.

He was still looking at her lovingly when she looked up from where her chair had moved. Meanwhile, Mwanga was expecting her to say something.

"Oh, thank…thank you," Monde finally got it.

"You're welcome," Mwanga accepted her gratitude.

Mwanga got another chair and sat down so that they both faced the same direction. They sat there gazing at the empty blackboard. They said nothing to each other for a while. And it was Monde who broke the silence.

"I thought that you were a bad guy."

"Me? Not really. I can be a good guy," Mwanga defended himself.

"I think I can accept your lunch today," Monde said.

No sooner had Monde expressed her intention than Mwanga pressed a special speed dial. Within twenty minutes or less, a van arrived with an assortment of Monde's favorite delicacies from Lusaka Fried Chicken (LFC). LFC was Monde's favorite restaurant.

But how did he know that I love LFC? Monde thought.

The two ate the food in silence. When they had finished, Mwanga said, "Thank you for accepting lunch from me."

"I must be thanking you, not the other way round," Monde said.

With the ice broken, the two conversed for at least thirty minutes. Monde learned that Mwanga thought she was different from all the other girls he had met.

"You struck me as someone familiar, though I've never actually met you," Mwanga revealed.

"As for me," began Monde, "You repulsed me the first time I saw you."

"But why?" Mwanga protested.

"I hate pompous people. They remind me of the devil," Monde was direct.

"Am I one, like the devil thing?" Mwanga teased.

Monde turned and looked intently at Mwanga. For the first time, their eyes met. They both withdrew rather quickly. It was dramatic as if it had been choreographed. They were smitten with each other's faces but not romantically. It was beyond normal. There was something about each other's eyes that was impossible to describe but easily felt. They both, almost simultaneously, felt like they were being transformed into some familiar dimension.

"I must be leaving now. Thanks for the food," Monde said as she gathered her personal effects and stood up.

"I should be thanking you again for accepting…"

Even before Mwanga finished his sentence, Monde was already gone. Mwanga sank into the chair and could not understand what had happened. That night, both Mwanga and Monde could not sleep.

[4] THE BOSS IN JAIL

The walls were made of bricks and mortar, fashioned from colonial labor during the Federation of Rhodesia and Nyasaland. The exterior presented itself as a magnificent fortress, featuring a high barbed-wire fence and gigantic floodlights that could reveal even the most camouflaged serpent.

It had the highest level of security of any prison in Zambia. It was the only prison in the country with double-fenced security. Even before one reached the walls, there was an invisible electric fence that, if breached, triggered an alarm. After the outer wall, there were cameras all around the prison. It was impossible to escape from Mukobeko Prison.

The name "Mukobeko" itself was derived from a term meaning "self-kill," or to commit suicide by hanging. One United Nations official who visited it for a fact-finding mission to assess Zambia's compliance with Resolution 34567, "The State of Human Rights in African Prisons," described it as the Alcatraz of Africa.

No one was officially known to have escaped from Mukobeko Prison. There was once a rumor that a prisoner attempted to escape and was bitten by electric snakes. Whether this was a myth or reality, no one knew. What was certain, however, was that the prison's security had not been compromised or breached because of that rumor.

Mukobeko Prison housed some of the most notorious criminals the nation had ever known from pedophiles to bank robbers, multimillion-dollar fraudsters, political insurrectionists, and drug dealers to traffickers. But no one came close to The Boss. He ruled the inside of the prison.

He had an entire hostel dedicated to serving him. He controlled the drug business inside the prison, killing before investigating and only investigating later. Yet, no one could link him to the deaths inside or outside the prison. He ruled with terror, and it was rumored that he had more money than the entire treasury of Zambia.

The Boss wore only khaki shorts and khaki T-shirts. No one had ever seen him in a suit. He was a vegetarian, having stopped eating meat during his incarceration at Southern Rhodesia Penitentiary (SRP) in Zimbabwe, where he was forced to kill and eat his colleague for the entire duration of his imprisonment. Meat reminded him of his colleague, and had it not been for Dr. Phiri, everyone around him would have thought he was going mad. He still suffered from nightmares and, because of that, never went to bed without drinking whiskey.

Every morning, he paid tribute to the
dead colleague he was forced to kill and eat
by sending out food and clothing to
inmates who had no families or relatives
outside of the prison. So, he was loved as
much as he was feared. He was kind as
much as he was ruthlessly brutal.

***

During Christmas and New Year, he
donated over US$50,000 to help street kids
all over Zambia, doing so incognito.
However, many street kids volunteered to
distribute drugs for the "Invisible Hand,"
as they called him. There were no rival
cartels in Zambia; there was only the
Arrogance Cartel. All others were merely
tributaries and subsidiaries. Leaders of
these tributaries and subsidiaries were
frequently arrested, interrogated, and
tortured, but none ever revealed who the
Invisible Hand was. Those who died while
being tortured either shouted or whispered,
"Lola," which meant "long live
Arrogance."

"Boss, he's here," whispered

Shokashoka, whose real name was Benjamin Kalasa. He, too, had been forced to eat human flesh at SRP. He acquired the nickname Shokashoka because he had perfected the art of torture using electric voltage. A former soldier, he was The Boss's most trusted bodyguard and was the only one who handled The Boss's food, including testing it before The Boss ate it. He also selected the whiskey for The Boss every night before The Boss went to bed.

"Let him in," The Boss said.

The Boss's room was a 17 by 20-foot self-contained palace-like enclosure. It had internet, a TV, and a double bed for The Boss. The room featured an ensuite washroom adorned with golden oriental embroideries. It looked more like a presidential suite than a prison cell.

The son entered.

It felt like a reunion, even though they had met just last month. It was evident that father and son shared a bond stronger than life itself. They hugged and remained in each other's arms for at least seven seconds.

"Welcome back, Son," the father said.

"Thank you, Dad," the son responded.

The Boss then motioned for everyone to leave him and his son alone. Pointing at Shokashoka, The Boss said, "Not you, Benjamin. You stay."

"Sure, Boss," Shokashoka replied.

The three enjoyed some snacks and light food that had been prepared for the occasion. As the conversation became awkward, the father and son almost spoke at the same time.

"I have something to tell you, Dad…" began the son.

"I called you here because…" the father started to speak but couldn't finish because the son had begun talking.
"Go on, Dad. Mine can wait."

"Sure, Son. Benjamin and I feel it's time to act on that project we mentioned to you last year. We're almost certain it will succeed."

"I trust you, Dad, but have you figured out how to navigate the electric fence? That seemed to be the toughest obstacle last time we talked."

"For that, I'll let Benjamin speak. Benjamin, go ahead."

Benjamin then shared a brilliant plan, taking ten to fifteen minutes to lay it out. The son was very impressed.

"And who came up with this plan?" the son asked, directing his question towards his father.

"I did, Son."

"Wow, I am speechless. This, too, from your dreams?"

"You bet, Son. But this one was more like a trance. I was reclining right there when I dozed off," The Boss said, pointing with a sense of resignation towards the area behind where Shokashoka was seated.

There was a momentary lapse before anyone said anything. The son removed what looked like a ledger from his pocket and handed it personally to his father. Taking it proudly, the father signaled to Shokashoka to hand him his reading glasses. After adjusting his glasses and reading only the last page, The Boss shook his head in bewilderment.

"Even I couldn't make sense of these numbers. Look, Benjamin," The Boss said, handing the piece of paper to Shokashoka.

"Maybe the prison has been the best thing that ever happened to you, Boss, in terms of business," Shokashoka said excitedly.

"I'm beginning to believe so. Son, you've exceeded expectations. The empire is now yours to rule. And how are you managing school and business?"

"It's been simple, Dad. In my private lessons, I've learned that delegation is like the ninth tentacle of an octopus."

"That statement right there says it all," the father said, relaxing.

"But…"

"But what, Son?"

It was the first time Mwanga Bwembya had hesitated to tell his father what was in his heart. He struggled to find the right words, knowing that once he indicated he had something pressing, his father would want to know at all costs.

"What did you say?" The Boss, Boss Boy's father, slumped over his desk. It was the first time the father was about to signal disapproval of his son's proposal. It wasn't because of his son's conversion to Christianity or his falling in love for the first time in his life. It was because the son had indicated that his conscience had begun to trouble him.

"You're trying to leave wealth and power because of a girl, Mwanga?" the father reiterated.

Mwanga knew not to answer his father when he was angry, so he kept silent. It took a while for The Boss to calm down. As Mwanga had expected, his father eventually did.

"You can have the girl, the... what's this..." The Boss beckoned to Shokashoka to complete his sentence.

"...born again..." Shokashoka suggested.

"Yes, fine. And you can still make money and manage the business as you are doing, Son."

"But Dad..."

"But what, Son?"

"The business is booming, but it's a sin..."

At that moment, The Boss became irritated. He flipped the table, broke all the whiskey glasses on the shelf, and ranted uncontrollably. Shokashoka took Mwanga to the kitchen area to give The Boss time to cool off. The more-than-seventeen bodyguards fell silent; you could hear a pin drop.

Shokashoka reentered The Boss's chamber with a glass of water. The Boss rejected it and gestured for whiskey instead. The Boss sipped the alcohol and asked for more.

Then he said, "Call Mwanga back in." Mwanga walked in confidently but respectfully. He grabbed the only chair that hadn't been overturned in anger and said nothing.

"Sorry, Son. I…"

"You don't have to apologize, Dad," Mwanga interrupted.

"Can I meet the girl?"

"One day, you will definitely meet her, Dad."

[5] LAZARUS COME FORTH

" And he said, 'Lazarus, come forth!' And the dead man came out of his tomb. He was still wrapped in grave clothes, and he still stank, but he was alive!"

The congregation gave a huge standing ovation, with chants of "Hallelujah" and "Amen" resonating across the 20,000-seater auditorium.

"You may be a Christian, but you're still stinking if you're still entangled with the devil's minions. To be truly free, even while alive, you must leave behind all appearances of evil…"

As the message hit home, Mwanga felt it personally. He began to realize that he was like Lazarus—alive but still stinking.

"Surely, I have given my life to Christ, but dealing drugs is a stinky thing. I must tell my father that I'm quitting right away. But the last time I tried to quit, he got mad," Mwanga thought.

And, yes, you're here debating, "What should I do? Leave my stinky life or continue sinning?" Be like me, my friend. When 32 years ago I stood before God, I didn't care about the negative voices urging me to continue my filthy life. Unlike many of you here, mine was truly filthy. I drank heavily, did drugs, killed people, and even gave my lost child to the devil…"

Bishop Mwendashi's message pierced Mwanga like a razor. He started to feel as if his surroundings were spinning. He grabbed Mwamba Ndalama, the lead bodyguard on duty who had attended the service with him that Sunday morning. He was perspiring heavily.

"I want to go," he said.

"Yes, Boss. Let me text the driver to bring the vehicle to the entrance," Mwamba replied.

"No, I want to go there," Boss Boy pointed to the front of the church.

When Mwamba realized that his boss was trying to go in front of the congregation to ask the bishop to pray for him, he struck his boss' median nerve, sending him into a deep sleep.

"Sorry, Boss, I must do this or it would cause a turf war among the rival gangs if they heard about this weakness," Mwamba whispered to a subdued body of his boss.

***

When the Boss Boy woke up that afternoon, he found himself on his own bed in his bedroom.

"Melody, how did I get here?" Boss Boy

asked his most trusted servant.

"Mwamba brought you here, Young Master. He said that you were not feeling well."

"Call Mwamba to come here," Boss Boy ordered.

"He's already gone, sir, remember it's his afternoon off Sundays."

"Oh, I forgot. Can I have some warm milk to drink?"

"Immediately, sir."

Mwanga drunk his warm milk while still thinking about the Lazarus message he heard at the Grand Cathedral. Then there was a knock on the door.

"Who's it?" Mwanga asked.

"It's me, again, sir," Melody answered.

"What's it now?" Mwanga asked without expecting any response.

"It's Khalebb and Clement. They want to speak with you."

"Let them in."

Khalebb had an urgent message for Boss Boy. And all he did was whispering into his boss' ears, "The Big Boss is on the phone, sir."

Mwanga quickly picked up the call and pretended as if he was sick.

"Yes, Dad."

"I hear that you have cancelled the operation meetings twice now, everyone is worried about you, Son."

"Yes, Dad, I know. I have taken Panadol; I will be fine."

"Is there something you're not telling me, Son. I understand that you went to some sort of a religious place…"

"But who told you?" Mwanga interrupted his father.

"Should I tell that, you know I have eyes everywhere? Son."

Mwanga realized it was futile to hide anything from his father. He came clean and explained everything, including the message he had heard.

"But let me tell you, Son, our business is legitimate. We operate our real estate business, companies, and industries legally."

"Dad, our so-called businesses are just money laundering schemes, and our money is blood money and—"

"So, you think that there's clean money, Son?"

"Yes, Dad. The lady bishop said that anything not from God stinks."

The mention of a lady bishop piqued The Boss's interest.

"Did you say you attended the church with a lady bishop?"

"Yes, Dad."

"What's her name?"

"I heard everyone calling her Bishop Mwendashi..."

"Stop right there, Mwanga. Don't ever go to that church!"

The tone in The Boss's voice struck fear into Mwanga. He knew this was serious. But why would his father be so affected by the mention of Bishop Mwendashi? The thought began to trouble Mwanga.

"But why, Dad? Bishop Mwendashi is a holy woman who preaches things that speak to my heart."

"That woman is your... Listen, just do what I'm telling you. Stop going to that church."

"She's my what, Dad?"

"Never mind, Son. Religion doesn't make you rich. It's a heart, as you pointed out, but not a money thing."

"But Dad, the bishop is very rich; she even owns a personal plane. I was thinking that if I commit to religion, I'd make money cleanly. Think about it, Dad."

"Oh, my poor son. There's so much you don't understand. It's either one or the other—you can't have both, money and God. Even their book says so."

"You're wrong, Dad. Last week, even the president attended church. And there are so many rich people who come to—"

"Mwanga, so you've been going there every Sunday?"

"Sort of…"

"No wonder business is being neglected. Now I understand."

"But… Dad," Mwanga stammered.

"Son, let me tell you the truth. That woman is plain greedy and evil. You and I actually have a business. But her business is pretending to love people so she can milk them of their wealth and satisfy her own wantonness. Just observe—who benefits from the money people give? I can assure you it's perhaps just herself and her family. The message she preaches is her business. Yes, it moved your soul to ensnare you into her greedy cage."

"Dad, do you know her? You speak as if you do."

"Yes, no, Son. I just know the likes of her."

Mwanga sighed softly with relief when his father hung up the phone with a command to "return to work and carry on from where you left off."

The exchange with his father had a significant impact on Mwanga's mind. He felt as if a burden had been lifted from his shoulders. The guilt he had felt after

CHARLES MWEWA

listening to Bishop Mwendashi's sermon
seemed to have vanished.

"My father could be telling the truth.
But Monde, I can't leave her," he thought.
"Benjamin, we must hasten the project,"
The Boss advised his most faithful servant
and confidante.

"Does it have to do with the call you
just had, Boss?"

"Yes. And the longer I remain here, the
quicker I will lose my son."

"What did you learn, Boss? You seemed
very upset."

"Very, very upset, Benjamin, is an
understatement. It has to do with Buggie."

Benjamin recalled meeting two
inseparable lovers over thirty years ago.
The girl always wore buggy pants and was a
quintessential tomboy. No one had seen
her curves in reality except Mila, as Beatrice
preferred to call the General, known as The
Boss.

"She's Buggie, Benjamin," the General had introduced her to him.

Benjamin and his twin sister, Mirimba, had pledged fealty to the General, especially after a fallout with the Mother. After the Mother put a ransom on the General's head, he escaped to the Kalene Hills of northwestern Zambia, where he set up camp and recruited militias, training them in guerrilla warfare.

Both Benjamin and Mirimba had fled to the Kasumbalesa border near what was then Zaire. It was pure luck and coincidence that they reunited with the General, who was then nicknamed The Boss.

Mirimba had joined a brothel, and Benjamin worked as a bouncer at a prestigious local pub around the Kasumbalesa border town. The Boss, having met some Italian drug traffickers and entered into concessions with them for the drug trade, had visited Kasumbalesa where pure Mandrax was rumored to be sold.

When the Boss's team landed in Kasumbalesa, they took hostage of the Rajmpada Bar, the prestigious local pub where Benjamin worked. When Benjamin was arrested and brought before The Boss, they were all shocked when Benjamin shouted, "It's you, General? I can't believe it. I thought I'd never see you again," and broke into loud tears.

"Leave him alone!" The Boss commanded.

"This is Benjamin, my comrade in arms," he added.

The two embraced in front of everyone. From that day on, Benjamin became The Boss's understudy.

The reunion was cause for celebration. "Mirimba is right here in Kasumbalesa with me," Benjamin told The Boss. Upon learning that Mirimba worked as a prostitute, The Boss ransomed her by paying the Lotoya Salon, the brothel where she worked, an unspecified amount of money. Since then, she had served The Boss's hacienda as a senior cook.

The "Kasumbalesa Expedition," as Mr. Chiolito Mendocino, the Italian mafia delegation boss, called it, was a success. But when the group went to Zimbabwe in search of top-grade cocaine, the Italians turned on The Boss and his crew, reporting them to the Zimbabwean authorities at Kubulawayo. There, they were blindfolded and taken to an unknown prison where they were tortured day and night, including being fed human remains.

After nearly two years in that prison, seven of them set the prison on fire and attempted to escape. Three died in the fire, and two were fatally shot. Only the Boss and Benjamin made it back to Kalene Hacienda.

Out of the approximately one thousand militias and servants, only seventeen were found. The rest had deserted. Three brave women, including Melody Mbewe and

Monica Ndelele, assumed the role of guardians of the hacienda.

Mirimba Gowani joined them later. She had been sent to Lusaka to lay claim to the promise made by the governments of Zambia and Britain to Mumba Makayi Milando Bwembya and Zeibous Mukangalume.

When she arrived in Lusaka, she learned that The Boss was on the list of most-wanted criminals in central southern Africa. She ran back to warn the people of Kalene Hacienda but the journey was arduous. She spent four months traversing mountains, valleys, and wild animals before locating the hacienda.

"What about Buggie now, Boss? Didn't you pay her the hush money?" Benjamin sought clarification.

"Benjamin, I knew she'd be greedy. Do you know it was she and Zeibous who identified us?"

"How do you know, sir?"

"John Lupembe."

"You mean the Director of Public Prosecutions?"

"Yes, that's him, the very same DPP."

"But how, Boss? Wasn't it his office that put us here?"

"That's right. Mwanga and his team kidnapped his family, and capitulated. He's now in our pockets, and I wanted to tell you but for Mwanga's love antics."

"Oh, does it mean he knows about our intentions to escape?"

"He's the one providing the intel. All things being equal, he'll deliver us out of these bars."

"I hope so, Boss."

"Me too, Benjamin."

[6] THE DILEMMA

“ Thanks for meeting me, Mr. Lupembe. I hope you enjoyed both the card and the gift?” It was a rhetorical question, and John Lupembe was not required to answer it. He stared in shock at the person seated at the back of the helicopter. He couldn't believe that the person Prisoner #432376 had been praising incessantly as the Patron of his drug cartel while he was absent was just a teenager.

“He should be, if I'm guessing right, just about 19 or early 20,” DPP John Lupembe thought.

"Are you going to receive the Patron's welcome, sir?" Matafwali Kalonji, the pilot, whispered into the DPP's right ear. The DPP was seated on the left front side of the pilot in a greyish Soviet-engineered helicopter. He was still holding the strap of the left stretch of the seatbelt, which he had been able to stretch completely into the buckle on his right-side pelvic angle.

"No, yes, sir," the DPP, just awakening from a temporary stupor, looked straight at the pistol brandished against him by Matafwali. Unknown to the DPP at that moment was that he was also looking at the man, the subject of a cold case he had worked on ten years ago when he was the Deputy DPP.

Ten years ago, the Zambian government had procured US$1.4 billion worth of ammunition from France. When it arrived in Zambia, the government pilot tasked with transporting the consignment from Lusaka to Mbala, the national armory in Northern Province, had gunned down seven soldiers assigned to escort him and diverted the aircraft carrying the

96

ammunition. They found the soldiers' remains at Nampungwe Airstrip near Mbala, but no sign of Matafwali or the aircraft was ever detected. Matafwali's name and the names of those dead soldiers remained classified, never released to the public. The DPP had never met Matafwali in person, although he knew him very well through photographs.

"I know this pilot, but from where?" a troubling thought crossed the DPP's mind.

As he sat, the three flew over towards the Kafue Gorge. During all this time, both the Patron Boy and Matafwali said nothing. Except for an occasional smile from the Patron Boy whenever the DPP looked at the back of the helicopter, the DPP seemed to be caught between the shock of seeing a teenage drug boss and the familiar face in his memory on his right-hand side.

"I think I remember him. This must be Matafwali Kalonji, the Concordia Killer!" The DPP thought and smiled.

He was not smiling out of amusement, but more out of shock at the discovery. Since neither the plane carrying the ammunition nor Matafwali was found, many conspiracy theories had arisen, from accusations that the Democratic Republic of Congo (DRC) had hijacked the plane and killed the soldiers, to the theory that the pilot was taken at gunpoint and thrown into the Indian Ocean. The main suspect had always been Matafwali, especially after a radio transmission intercepted seemed to capture Matafwali's voice saying, "See you in hell," followed by three gunshots.

The helicopter landed in the middle of nowhere in the deep jungles of the Kafue Forest. Quickly, five armed men approached and saluted the Patron Boy, who instructed them to "take him to see his family."

The reunion with his wife and two girls was cut short when another armed man arrived and took the DPP away.

"You wanted proof of life? There you had it," the armed man said.

The DPP was taken into a Land Rover on a gravel road to an unknown location, blindfolded. As they left, he heard his wife screaming as they were taken into another Land Rover, he had seen parked.

"Where are they taking them?" the DPP asked the armed man seated next to him.

"Somewhere safe. Don't worry."

"When will I see them again?"

"When the mission is over, I guess."

"But…" The DPP tried to speak.

"Keep your questions to yourself. Address them to the Patron soon," the armed man spoke with an emotionless sense of finality.

There were still many unanswered questions in his head, such as why he was not blindfolded when they took him in a helicopter to meet his family, how the Patron Boy had left that place, as the greyish helicopter was still parked when they departed, and why they had to move his family again.

"We meet again, Mr. Lupembe. Let me now introduce myself properly. My name is…"

"Matafwali Kalonji, the Concordia Killer. I worked on your case for years. Everyone thought you were dead, but somehow knew you were alive," the DPP interrupted.

"Oh, wow, you've got a good memory. So, there is no need for further introductions. But let me introduce you to The Team…"

"But out of curiosity, I have always wanted to know how you did it. Can I have the pleasure of knowing?" The DPP asked about how the Concordia Killer pulled it off and disappeared.

There was a long pause. Matafwali smiled and said, "There will be time for that. First, first things first."

"This is the time, I insist. I may not come out of this trap alive. At least let me have my death wish," the DPP begged.

"What do you think? I did it on a hunch."

"Unaided?" The DPP asked.

"No, it was a solo mission."

"Like Kingsley Chinkuli?"

"Worse, I think," The Concordia Killer answered.

"And this organization, it's grander than Adamson Mushala?" The DPP gestured, making it a rhetorical question.

"Couturier than Comrade Mushala's, but inspired by it," The Concordia Killer said softly.

Then Matafwali signaled that there would be no further questions. The Team gathered. It comprised Matafwali, the pilot, Katuta Chembe, the bomb expert, Dorothy Mvula, the liaison enchanter, Morgan

Mulopwe, the negotiator, and Nalumino Pemba, the impersonator. The only missing link was an authoritative figure to arrange the transfer of The Boss from Mukobeko Prison to Chimbokaila Maximum Security Prison (CMSP). The plan was to kidnap the DPP and his family to force him to arrange the transfer.

> We hope this to be a quick, bloodless operation. The DPP will force the transfer via The Path. This route is known only to the elite of the Zambia Intelligence Service (ZIS), and the DPP is one of them, along with the ZIS director and the Attorney General. We decided to use the weakest link, the DPP. My father will threaten to kill the Prison Warden at Mukobeko Prison, which will provoke a transfer to CMSP. As you know, General Dadafi Mwale, the warden of Mukobeko, is President Zeibous' uncle. The transfer will be approved easily by the president. Is there anything I've left out, Mr. Lupembe?

"Just one detail, Mr....Mr...." The DPP shuddered.

"It's the Patron, Mr. Lupembe," Katuta Chembe corrected him.

> Thanks. As I was saying, Mr. Patron, the escape will happen on Heroes and Unity Day. The police force is usually stretched to capacity limits, and The Path is open for VIP movements. I have paid the reconnaissance troupe leader to redirect the presidential motorcade and give us a thirteen-minute window to strike on The Boss' convoy and rescue him.

"But don't you think that snipers will be all over The Path during this time?" Nalumino Pemba asked.

Then the DPP responded:

> Don't forget that I double as Secretary of ZIS. The Path is a classified national secret. Only open routes are disclosed to the public and the media, and snipers are positioned in those open routes. There is only ground reconnaissance in The Path to avoid alerting would-be assassins.

"Everything clear now?" The Patron Boy asked.

Everyone nodded that it was clear, but the Patron wanted to make sure. So, he went through the list one by one.

"Matafwali?"

"Yes, Patron."

"Nalumino?"

"Sure, Patron."

"Katuta?"

"Indeed, Boss."

"Dorothy?"

"Patron!"

"And you, Morgan?"

"Very clearly, Boss."

"Everyone, leave, except you, Mr. DPP," ordered the Patron Boy.

After everyone had left, the Patron Boy turned to the DPP and asked if he could confirm having received the "gift."

"Yes, I did, but it's too good to be true, sir."

"Well, what's the problem?"

"It's in my name for sure, but it's too big, sir."

"Well, it must be, because as you may be aware, Dad's empire is now richer than the Zambian economy."

"What will happen to my family, sir, and…"

"And what, Mr. DPP?"

"And what if I want to join, being a permanent part of this empire?"

"Well, you have to pass a test and swear an oath of fealty!"

"When can I do both?"

"Well, this is your test: deliver Dad out safely, and then you can take the oath!"

"Deal, Patron, sir!"

"Deal."

***

It was an extended stretch of about 30 kilometers passing right under one of the nation's grandest and best-protected national parks, Kafue National Park.

The tunnel itself was about eight meters wide and eight meters high, with a well-maintained gravel surface and an impressive array of lights flooding the way like a starry canopy.

Sound absorbers were mounted on a canvas of extremely porous concrete so that no matter how loud the noise underneath, no one or no mechanical sound detection device could detect it on the upper surface.

The DPP sat there underground in a fully armored Toyota Land Cruiser 200, sandwiched between two other fully armored vehicles: an Ineos Grenadier in front and a Lexus LX 500 at the back. All the vehicles were black Sports Utility Vehicles (SUVs).

He was told that a communication center had been established to monitor the interior and exterior of the tunnels.

"As you can see, we know even when the ZIS director himself is going to the toilet," Lufungulo Lwitunde, the driver of the Toyota armored SUV, explained.

All the DPP could do was shake his head in wonder. He sank into deep thought. "It's no wonder they say he is more powerful than the president. Now I know why. He rules this nation."

After close to 30 minutes, they emerged into another forest where a boat was waiting for them. They traveled on the river for about 25 minutes and disembarked onto another armored silvery Range Rover SUV. During the speedboat trip, the Team did not speak to each other.

When they settled into the Range Rover, the Patron Boy asked the DPP a rhetorical question, "What do you think, lawman? Can you rate your ride experience?"

Everyone in the vehicle broke into loud laughter. The DPP was surprised to see that as they traveled by road, several villagers, whom he learned were trained militias and workers of the Arrogance Cartel, lined the paved gravel roads to welcome the Patron Boy.

Some people brought small lunchbox-like bowls to hand to the Patron's bodyguard, Khalebb, who was waiting in the SUV with Mo and the driver when the Team disembarked from the river. Khalebb picked up the bowls and handed them over to Mo, who put them in a cooler. This process was repeated several times until they arrived at the operation camp at Kalene Ranch.

"Mo, let me know the grades tomorrow morning. I'm going to bed," the Patron Boy ordered.

"Yes, Patron!"

When they retired to bed that evening, the DPP and the Patron Boy had different opinions. The DPP could hardly believe his luck that day.

When he woke up the next morning, he lay motionless in bed, trying to process all that had happened the previous day.

The DPP reflected:

> *I studied the law to become rich using the rule of law, but it turns out there's a quicker way to wealth. We corrupt government officials to gain power and riches, but here's a man, or his boy, who works smartly, albeit unlawfully, and possesses billions in real property and power.*
>
> *And that revelation has shaken my mind. All the Blue Gym franchises are his, the Fungulu Mall in Kabulonga, the nation's largest shopping center, is his, the newly built Kasama International Airport in Lusaka West is his, the...*

A soft knock on the door interrupted the DPP's thoughts.

"Yes, you may enter."

It was Khalebb.

"The Patron invites you for breakfast, sir."

They ate breakfast in a relatively calm and quiet atmosphere. The Patron Boy was patient, very friendly, and welcoming.

"So, did you have a change of mind overnight, Mr. Lupembe?"

"Yes, but in a positive way. I am very impressed. You have brought more development while operating in the shadows than we who run the public governance system. I am truly flabbergasted, in a happy way, you understand?"

"Yes, I do."

"We just need to bring Daddy home, you hear me?"

"On my life and the life of the three most precious gifts of my family, sir!" The DPP, Mr. Lupembe, promised.

"By the way, your family is at home. They are also enjoying an extra $20,000 to spend as we speak."

"But… but aren't they afraid to…?"

"Huh… you're thinking about misgivings, fear, and grudges? No, there aren't any because you spoke to them."

"But how? I haven't spoken to them since two days ago, and I didn't say much…"

> Except asking how they were feeling, I know. But you spoke to them yesterday afternoon through your AI Alvaro voice. They heard that you were voluntarily cooperating with us to make a better world for Zambia. You even sent them $20,000.00, video games for the children, and an in-house massage therapist for your wife. They were also instructed not to say anything to anyone, except that you were still enjoying your vacation. Our eyes on and near your house reported that your family is the happiest it has ever been.

The DPP was silent for some time, processing all that had just been disclosed to him. The Patron Boy started to worry that he might not be pleased with what they had done for his family. Then, all of a sudden, the DPP burst into tears of joy.

"Can I hug you, Sir?" the DPP asked, and without waiting for a response, he was all over the Patron Boy's neck, hugging and kissing him.

Khalebb wanted to draw his grey Glock 18 pistol, but the Patron winked clandestinely as if to say to his bodyguard, "Don't worry, everything is okay."

The next morning, Mwanga had returned to Lusaka for a physics exam. He was back to being the Boss Boy.

It was Friday.

Mwanga had invited Monde to his house in Lusaka West. Monde knew that Mwanga came from a wealthy family based on his power and how he presented himself at school, but she had no idea that his wealth was unmatched by anyone she had ever known.

"Wow, Darling, don't tell me you live here?" It was a rhetorical question; she already knew the answer.

"Yes, it's a small part of it," he said nonchalantly.

"This small? You're kidding me!" Monde exclaimed. It was like a dream.

Seventeen women, including a massage therapist, a manicure-pedicure specialist, a fashion designer, a professional photographer, a dietitian, a singer, and a musician, were all at her disposal.

She had no time to be with Mwanga anymore. She tried hard to get to him, asking twice in a span of two hours, "Where's Mwanga?"

No one seemed to care. It looked like they had strict instructions to pamper her to the fullest.

When evening came and Monde wanted to go home, Mwanga entered the room where Monde was sitting and admired her new self. Seeing him, she jumped on him and began to kiss him all over. He, meanwhile, motioned for everyone to leave the room.

"Oh, you're shy, Boss Boy, you're being defeated by a woman," Monde teased him, pinning him down on a couch.

"I have never, you know, kissed a girl before," Mwanga disclosed.

"Neither have I. But today we have," Monde said, bringing her lips closer to his.

Before they could blink, their lips had interlocked, their tongues wrapping around each other, their breathing becoming erratic.

They kissed for more than seven minutes before instinctively withdrawing. Each cowered into a corner, mumbling to oneself, "N-o, n-o, no-t no-w."

Shyly, they came together, hugging tightly, squeezing out all the passion they had experienced. Breathing a deep sigh of relief, they let each other go.

Monde picked up her handbag and left the room quietly. Mwanga dropped onto the floor, staring at the ceiling.

Monde approached her chauffeured car near the main entrance. Looking back at Mwanga, she whispered to herself while blowing a gentle kiss in his direction, "*Lord, I thank you for giving me a rare gift,*" she prayed.

Monde and Mwanga were in love and in Christ. They woke up sending each other kisses through emojis and leaving prayers through voice memos. Monde talked about Mwanga to her staff constantly, and Mwanga's every waking moment was occupied with thoughts of Monde.

It was first Maureen who remarked when Mwanga asked her about Monde that they were "a match made in heaven, even the way you two talk and look."

Monde heard it from Gertrude.

"My Lady, for sure, you are truly the Holy Girl."

"Why do you say so?"

"God does answer prayers, I know. But the way He answered yours is nothing short of a miracle. Your resemblance to your boyfriend is amazing. It's like you're Mary, the mother of Jesus."

The two laughed until they fell asleep. Monde took it as a compliment, her smile never fading as she thought about Mwanga.

Meanwhile, the Team struggled to reach Mwanga. They had gone the entire week without him showing up at the daily briefing. Matafwali had resumed the role of the Team leader, but even Matafwali couldn't stop the secret actions of the "eyes" from reaching The Boss in prison.

"Look, Benjamin, Mwanga has been spooked by a girl. He can't even pay attention to the task at hand," The Boss roared.

"It seems like it's Mila and Buggie again, Sir," Benjamin joked.

"Was it like that… with us… I mean?"

"Even worse, Sir."

"Really?"

"I bet it, Boss."

"No wonder I went for castration when I lost her. I sometimes remember her when I see her preaching on TV."

"I know. I notice it too. But you have done well, Sir, without women, the weakest link in all human failures."

"Indeed. But whiskey can be just like women. You wake every morning with the resolve not to drink ever again but end up sipping it at the slightest desire."

"But it doesn't concern the heartiest matters, and besides, it takes only one person down. But…"

Benjamin was interrupted:

I know, Benjamin. Women make strong men piss themselves off and then realize afterward that it was a lost cause. It will be the same with the boy, but I can't stop that. He's young, full of energy, and his John doesn't stop barking. That's why I had mine chopped off, and you followed suit.

"I remember, Boss. And look at what we did after that, establishing an empire that is far richer than the entire Central African economies combined."

"Yep, it is, Benjamin. But I need to take control of the project before Mwanga ruins it with his infatuations. Arrange a call."

"Sure, straight away, Sir."

"Dad, this is all I can report right now. Business was slow because of..." Mwanga was interrupted by his father.

"Mwanga, I am reliably told that you didn't attend the weekly meetings, not even once?"

"It's true, Dad, I wasn't feeling well."

"Again…" The Boss began.

Just then, a security officer whispered in his ear, "Time has been extended four times, Boss. I will get in trouble with the deputy warden if I extend it again."

Reluctantly, The Boss said goodbye to his son.

When he reached his club-like cell, The Boss beckoned to his bodyguard, "We must expedite the escape. Tell the crew here to contact the Team outside and prepare."

"What should I tell the team about timing, Boss?" the bodyguard asked.

"In three weeks."

The bodyguard was shocked but could not say or show it.

"I can't wait any longer. The boy seems tied and, at his age, he has done well, but… I must escape and protect the business," The Boss muttered to himself.

When the Boss had summoned his internal crew of bodyguards and prison officers on his payroll, he announced, "I have the final piece of the puzzle."

He then turned to Shokashoka and ordered, "Call Mwanga and tell him to come and see me tomorrow morning, in person."

"Your word is my command, Boss," Shokashoka accepted.

Early the next morning, Mwanga visited the prison. What was discussed between him and The Boss was kept a secret.

When Mwanga left the prison, he was deep in thought:

> I am loving this Jesus and Monde, but I must still fulfill my father's wish. What if I decide to no longer be part of the business, or I do it with them now, and when my father is rescued, I stop?

Mwanga left the prison premises and was driven to meet Monde.

"Boss, Nalumino Pemba did it. She impersonated Mr. Ndhlovu and delivered a coup de grace," Benjamin reported.

Benjamin had woken up feeling dejected because his and The Boss's hopes of escaping prison had been dashed by the Deputy DPP's exposure of part of the scheme with the Team. He had gotten the DPP's daughter arrested and interrogated. The child had disclosed that The Boss had used his outside-of-prison network to kidnap her, her sister, and her mother.

When she was where they were held, she said without blinking, "I don't know. We would sleep, then wake up in a different place. The place had no windows, no TVs, and no visible landmarks. We were given books to read and plenty of computer games to play."

When she was probed further and told that "your father was arrested and revealed that he worked for the Arrogance Cartel," she felt compelled to say what happened.

"I don't think he worked with them because he was allowed to see us only once, and when he saw us, he was in tears. Dad never cried until it concerned our safety," she said.

"So, is he still on vacation?" Ndhlovu had inquired.

"No, I don't think so. I think they cut his vacation short and kidnapped him. He must be in pain or he is dead already."

"Why do you say so?"

"Because Dad would never abandon us," she said.

Ndhlovu had gone ahead and implicated his boss in a conspiracy to break The Boss out of prison. He particularly used the instructions his boss had given him to transfer the Boss from Mukobeko to Chimbokaila during the H&U Day as a ploy to exploit the vulnerability of the intelligence service during that time.

President Zeibous was briefed, and he ordered the Minister of Home Affairs, Father Winston Bupe, to transfer The Boss to an unknown location, where The Boss would have no visiting privileges. His most trusted right-hand man, Benjamin Kalasa, was transferred to Chimbokaila.

.

[7] THE PATH

It was built during the Adamson Mushala rebellion. With the aid of traditional magic, Mushala could enter and leave the State House undetected at will. According to classified documents, he once spent three days wearing President Kenneth Kaunda's pajamas and hung his jacket at the president's breakfast table for an entire week.

When all efforts to contain the elusive Mushala failed, the Zambian government constructed a prison specifically to hold him if he was ever captured. This prison was built from solid concrete blocks and metal bars. It measured four by four by six meters and had a tiny hole allowing for sunlight for only fifteen minutes each day.

Food was passed through a 30 by 15-centimeter slot in a drywall that snapped back into place once released. The facility was equipped with 47 cameras positioned strategically throughout the area, and the toilet infrastructure was electronically controlled to detect any foreign substances in both feces and urine.

There were no windows, and it contained a half-twin bed with only a rubber sheet—no mattress. The prisoner had to learn to sleep straight without bending.

Light was on for only six hours each day. It was designed so that if a prisoner survived three months in it, they would either become deranged or impotent. It had been seven months since The Boss was held in the State House prison.

When the prisoner physician examined him, the report, which was also made available to President Zeibous, read as follows: "He's in good spirits and excellent health. He has shown no signs of derangement, and his mental capacity has been improving or remained steadfast."

When asked by the Secretary to the Cabinet, Dr. Perry Mwitwa stated, "His remarkable resilience is owed to his vegetarian lifestyle and his castration."

Statehouse security council chairwoman, Feby Muluti, was asked about the likelihood of his escape and said, "Even James Bond wouldn't be able to breach this impenetrable fortress."

The Boss woke up around 5:59 a.m. in his orange jumper labeled #000002, the second person to be imprisoned there. The only other prisoner who had spent time in the facility was Lt. Mwamba Luchembe, Prisoner #000001, who had been held for only four days. Adamson Mushala, for whom the prison was originally built, had been killed in the field and never had a chance to be incarcerated there.

"I must exercise more now, because my redemption draws near," he spoke loudly enough to be heard by the security staff, who analyzed every day what the prisoner said and did not say. They were puzzled as to why, after six months and two weeks of silence, he had spoken now and why he seemed upbeat.

The ten-member statehouse prison council deliberated for hours, developing various theories. However, they all agreed that Prisoner #000002 was planning an escape.

"But why announce it?" one council member wondered.

"And why, after six months of model behavior, is he now feeling the impact of solitary confinement?" another questioned. "He seemed upbeat and deliberate," a third member observed.

By the end of the meeting, they decided to tighten outside security and place reinforcements around the perimeter. They also agreed to increase daylight hours to twelve.

When the resolution reached President Zeibous' office, he simply remarked, "You must tighten security; General can be very slippery." His tone was matter-of-fact, and it did not raise any alarms. The report proceeded, and other matters took precedence, leaving the situation unchanged.

It was around 5 p.m. on an October Saturday. The afternoon had been notoriously hot, with temperatures reaching over 30°C. The early evening brought heavy humidity, and many electric cars were parked that day. Numerous celebrations and parties took place to take advantage of the northeasterly winds that provided some relief.

The first bomb exploded around 5:07 p.m. at the exit of the Path. Five motorcades were escorting the Vice-President, Madam Gabriella Munalula. A recon officer had redirected the VIP motorcade to retreat. Just as it was nearing central Path, around 5:23 p.m., another bomb exploded at the entrance of the Path. Ground rescue of the stranded VIPs became impossible. President Zeibous ordered the activation of the National Emergency Act (NEA), granting the Zambian Airforce authority to rescue the stranded VIP motorcade.

At first, the government had no intention of broadcasting the events due to the classified nature of the Path. However, social media quickly became inundated with images of destruction and reports of "The destruction of the clandestine escape route Zambian politicians created to facilitate corrupt transactions," according to Mwebantu, an online news media outlet.

By around 5:57 p.m., all aircraft flying near or along the Path began to crash as their fuel began to freeze. This phenomenon was unprecedented, prompting the Zambian Defence Council (ZDC) to convene at State House that evening to deliberate on the Path rescue and the way forward. The nation was anxiously awaiting news from its leaders.

At exactly 5:59 p.m., a loud noise echoed through the State House compound, followed by an eerie silence. The ZDC in session initially found some comfort in the fact that the noise was not an explosion into the air but rather something akin to a sinking ship—roaring once and then fading away.

Then, a military security officer stationed near the East Gate towards the State House Prison (SHP) burst into the council chamber and collapsed on the floor. He was quickly resuscitated. Once he regained his composure, his first words were, "It's no longer there."

The council's chairman, the president, asked, "What's not there?"

The panicked officer pointed toward the SHP and said, "The prison, Your Excellency."

"Everything is ready, Boss." Mumba Makayi Milando Bwembya, nicknamed "the Boss," had hardly settled when one of his bodyguards, known as "Babs," at Chimbokaila Maximum Prison (CMP), called him to visit the infirmary. The plan had been fifteen years in the making. Since its establishment in the 1960s, CMP had been home to the country's most notorious criminals, and no one had ever escaped.

"You packed my bag—the one with the two inner layers?"

"Yes, Boss," Babs replied, without meeting the Boss's gaze.

Dr. Mukelabai, Zambia's most renowned plastic surgeon, had performed a unique surgery on himself—a measure he was compelled to undertake to save his kidnapped family, who were currently held in an unknown location. Only Dr. Mukelabai, Babs, Fube, and the Boss knew about this operation. Both Babs and the Boss were still serving their sentences of 35 and 42 years, respectively, within the prison.

Outside, Fube, known among gangs as "The Arrogant," had been tasked with a crucial role. Two months before, at the Boss' request, Fube had kidnapped Dr. Mukelabai when he was about to enter his compound. After disabling the automatic gate, Fube had seized Dr. Mukelabai and his family at gunpoint and taken them to their current location.

"Mom, this is Mwanga, my boyfriend," Monde announced to Bishop Mwendashi.

What followed was a meeting and introduction of the complex to Mwanga.

Mwanga had asked about 200 questions regarding everything from the complex's structure to the Bishop's routines and the security measures.

"We must stay the weekend *here*. I want to read more about God in the library," Mwanga said to Monde.

When Monde relayed this to her mother, her mother was thrilled, "Finally, you've found a godly man, Darling. He's even better than you; he's willing to study about our Lord. Praise God."

"Mother…"

"What, my queen, am I not telling the truth?"

"No, Mother…"

As Monde was framing her next bluff, the bishop was in deep thoughts, *This boy, have we met somewhere?*

That weekend, Mwanga was active in the library and had two of his bodyguards, whom he had introduced to the complex as his "friends in need of a savior."

The First Bodyguard said, "We have the map, Young Master."

"Alright, guys, let's go!"

[8] THE ESCAPE

He had sat in the back row with his three bodyguards. Khalebb was seated immediately to his right, Clement to his left, and Chisanshi directly behind him. Boss Boy was lost in thought about the previous sermon preached by Bishop Mwendashi, titled "Jesus Came to Set Prisoners Free."

No wonder I am loving attending this church. Not only has it given me the sweet gift of Monde, but the bishop's messages are also so relevant. Jesus, I ask, please set my father free from prison, Boss Boy prayed thoughtfully.

The lights were turned on bright just after the praise and worship segment, which had lasted about 45 minutes. The last song, "Jesus Lover of My Soul," sung by the symphonic choir, had brought him to tears, which he had conveniently concealed. Just before tithes and offerings were collected, a lanky elderly man appeared on strategically placed television screens.

He introduced himself as Elder Mullen and delivered a stirring oratory to encourage the congregation to give generously.

"I am reading from Numbers 7:59," Elder Mullen began, "'And for a sacrifice of peace offerings, two oxen, five rams, five he-goats, five lambs of the first year; this was the offering of Nahshon the son of Amminadab.' Today's message invites us to give sacrificially according to how God has blessed us. Some have oxen blessings; others have ram blessings. Still others have goat blessings, and some may have lamb blessings. We're sons of God, and like Nahshon, we must give to…"

As Elder Mullen reached the crescendo of his oration, Boss Boy was breathing heavily, struck by a sudden idea. Amid the enthusiastic "Amen. Amen" cheers from the congregation, Boss Boy's excitement became uncontrollable. He stood up suddenly and shouted, "That's it!" His bodyguards quickly stood up with him, minimizing the attention he drew.

While his bodyguards assumed he was moved by the giving message, Boss Boy was energized by a revelation. He had been struggling to devise a plan to rescue his father from the impenetrable State House Prison. The Team looked to him for guidance as the acting leader of the Arrogance Cartel.

"God is good. He has finally given me what to say to the Team," he whispered to Khalebb.

"And was that the reason you stood up and shouted, Boss?" Khalebb asked, whispering back.

Without hesitation, Boss Boy replied, "Yes. Tell Chisanshi to put a generous offering in the basket for me."

"Yes, Boss. Is that to thank God for the idea you got from the message?" Khalebb asked.

"Yes. Tell everyone that we are leaving." The four left just as the congregation was asked to stand and offer a prayer for the offering.

Even before they could reach the library located in the basement of their Lusaka West ranch, Clement was ordered to send a message to the Team for an urgent meeting.

Around 3:00 p.m. that afternoon, Boss Boy unveiled what he called a "divine idea." "My Father in heaven has revealed a divine idea for rescuing my father on earth," he began. "Because His Son came to set prisoners free, it is my responsibility, as the son to my father, to set him free."

The speech pleased the Team, and thus "Operation 7:59" was born. According to the confession obtained from Ndhlovu, the operation involved kidnapping the families of the SHP executive director and the head of IT. Once the two complied, the Team would study the prison's design, construction, and operation. They would then investigate the routines of the SHP staff. Operation 7:59 involved building a tunnel directly to the SHP using highly sophisticated, soundproof equipment. Most of the work was done during the day when everyone was busy.

Exactly seven months after The Boss was transferred to SHP, and at the 59th minute of the seventh hour, the entire cage structure where The Boss was held would be carved out and transported through the tunnel to a secure location, where it would be opened to free The Boss. The tunnel would then be completely buried.

Operation 7:59 was executed to perfection.

The Boss was free.

"You called me, Mr. President? I was informed rather late," Bishop Mwendashi apologized.

"Yes, my personal secretary told me that you were not available."

"It's true. I was in a leadership meeting and…"

"No need for a detailed explanation. I understand."

"Thank you, Mr. President."

"But did you hear the news?"

"You mean about Bwembya's escape? Yes, I did."

"So, what do you think, Beatrice?"

She paused for a moment, cleared her throat, and then responded.

"Truth be told, Zeibous, he's still deceiving you, despite all the governmental power you wield. You know what this means, don't you?"

"I do. I am extremely worried, Beatrice. I am."

"You better be. I think that…"

"My chances of getting reelected have been jeopardized. I need your help again, Beatrice."

"Of course, I will help you—for our daughter's sake."

She sat alone in her study, which was across from her gigantic office. Her office was twice as large as that at State House. She remembered vividly when Zeibous had visited her office and remarked, "Beatrice, you accuse us in your sermons of corruption, and yet you are the one who is superfluous and materialistic."

She thought, *Yes, he was perfectly right. Look at me, alone, watching my own self become flappy in a self-inflicted abstinence prison.*

As she considered the opportunities she might have had if she had married him, she thought, "I knew he's a rebel and an outlaw, but he's the only man I have ever loved. Oh, Mother…"

She hastily called for her driver to take her to Old Leopard Hill Cemetery. Upon reaching the hill, she asked her bodyguard to buy some yellow flowers.

As she arranged the flowers on her mother's grave, she spoke silently to the tomb, "You thought you knew what was best for me. But you only subjected me to this unpleasant experience. I can't date, I can't be myself. My thoughts are constantly inhibited. I can't dance to good music or be sorrowful for fear of being judged unfaithful. So, I pretend to be better than others. I truly admire Monde. At least she can be who she is; not me."

She replaced the old, dry bouquet with a new one and dusted the epitaph placard that read, "Here lies Mother, the matriarch of our freedom." Then she kissed the stone and walked for almost fifteen minutes to reach her parked vehicle.

No sooner had she entered her vehicle than she received a call on the "other" phone. Devon Mumbi, who had recently been hired as her chauffeur, was unaware that when the "other" phone rang, no one was supposed to be near the bishop.

The bishop tried to gesture to Devon to leave her alone, but Devon thought she wanted him to drive off.

"Where to, Ma'am?" Devon asked.

Furiously, she raised her voice and shouted, "Get out of the car, leave me alone!"

Devon complied and left.

"Was that the 13th discipline herself losing it?" an authoritative voice questioned.

"I am sorry, Your Excellency. Anger got the best of me. You wanted to talk to me?"

"Yes, Beatrice. I think your preaching is needed to help us win over public opinion as you did last time."

"But the election is not until two years from now, Zeibous."

"No, it's not about the election, though I will discuss that with you in due course."

"Then, what is it?"

The president paused. His first private secretary brought him some water, but he declined. The secretary left.

"There's commotion. Mila's escape has caused tremendous public panic."

"He's not mine. I asked you not to kill him because I didn't want my son to grow up without a father."

"Have you even met your son? The last time you spoke about him was ten years ago. How old is he now?"

"He must be 21 years old now. No, I have never met him. I only have a photo…"

"You mean the same one that was sent to you by the intelligence agent?"

"Yes, that's right."

"I believe he's at Kabulonga High, where he's known as Boss Boy. My intelligence officers told me so."

"What, Zeibous? That's where your daughter transferred to!"

"I know. But we have the agreement…"

"I am aware that no one can ever know you are her father, or we will be discredited—both you by the electorate and me by the church."

What was critical was that the two should hide their pact, which stipulated that no harm should come to Bwembya and his son unless he decided to overthrow the government. Before his arrest and escape, The Boss had been distributing prohibited drugs to the public, and it was the bishop herself who had identified him.

"But..." Gwendolyn Kabaso, deputy minister of Home Affairs, had barely begun her report in Parliament when it was interrupted.

"But what, Madam Kabaso? You appeared in this august house nearly two and a half years ago and reassured the nation that apprehending The Boss of the Arrogance Cartel would rid our streets of gangs and drugs. But, hey, no, since his incarceration, street crimes and drug trafficking have only increased..."

The full house erupted into a standing ovation, with deafening applause.

Yussouf Banda, official opposition leader of the People's Party for Democracy (PPD), after calming the house, continued speaking,

> ...as I was saying, we were told that The Boss was a loner and putting him in the maximum-security prison would benefit our children, but it didn't. And for the record, Mr. Speaker, the

Arrogance Cartel was reported to be
the largest drug ring in Central Africa,
and now its leader is in prison. Can the
deputy minister in the Ministry of
Home Affairs explain to this house
and to the nation why that is so, and
who was in charge of the cartel while
its leader was incarcerated?

The noise was overwhelming. When it subsided, the deputy minister of Home Affairs spoke.

"Mr. Speaker, The Boss is no longer in prison. As you all know, his escape is the reason for this emergency National Assembly session. So, the question of who was in charge in his absence is redundant…"

"But it is not, Mr. Speaker," interrupted Mr. Banda, "…to many of us, the person who was in charge while The Boss was incarcerated is more dangerous than The Boss himself, because it means that the problem of drugs in this country will not end."

"Answer that question, Madam Kabaso, Hon. MP from Kamalonde Constituency, and deputy minister of Home Affairs," charged the Speaker, Mr. Kevin Hambolelwa.

"Mr. Speaker," the deputy minister of Home Affairs stood up, "...reliable sources have confirmed that it was a young man, probably in his late teens or early twenties, who led the Arrogance Cartel in The Boss's absence..."

"A *boy*, Mr. Speaker..."

Just before Mr. Banda could finish his speech, the Speaker hammered the gavel hard on the table and shouted, "Order! Order in the House! And for you, Mr. Banda, leader of the opposition PPD, you must allow the deputy minister to finish her speech."

From there, the house ceased making noise and adhered to the rules. The house learned that a young man had managed the multibillion-dollar empire in The Boss's absence.

The house also learned that the young man could be related to The Boss and could even be his only child. The deputy minister of Home Affairs pledged to "furnish the House with more accurate information in the next session," and the proceedings were adjourned.

"You understand, Zeibous, that our children are in the lion's den, right?"

"What do you mean, Beatrice?"

"Because anything can happen there. For example, they could discover that they are both my children. As you know, Mila is everything but a traitor; he never breaks his word."

"I know, Beatrice. During the last elections, I almost..."

"What, say it. What did you almost do?"

"I am sorry, Beatrice, but I even sent my men to eliminate him, but all they killed was a man who impersonated him. DNA proved it."

"Oh, you did that? But why? The man never challenged you, and in fact, he kept his word!"

"At the time, I had false intelligence that he was planning to expose me to the nation. It seemed imminent..."

"So?"

"But it turned out he actually kept his word. After we put him in prison, I doubt he'd protect us."

"What are you planning?"

"That's the reason I called you, Beatrice."

"No, no, *Zeib Muka*, you can't assassinate him."

"But he's mad, he's gone crazy. And you know that he's the only man alive who knows my weakness, including about our daughter."

"No, Mila..."

"Come on, Beatrice, don't call him by that name…"

"Why?"

"It reminds me…"

"Of what? That he was once my sweetheart whom you and Mother betrayed? That he was tricked into losing his love?"

"Relax, Beatrice, you…"

"Muka don't kill Mila, no matter what, or I will not help you win reelection. I am serious."

"Let's do this: if he continues to keep quiet and doesn't interfere with my reelection, I will not kill him. But if he shows any signs, I will. Fair?"

"Mhm… you are trying to play politics with me. You will kill him for any probable likelihood and then offer an excuse. I know you better."

"No, Beatrice. I will consult with you if it comes to that. Agreed?"

"Reluctantly, Zeib Muka."

The president and the bishop took heavy jabs at each other. It was clear that the synergy that had made them a team leading to electoral victory no longer existed.

The pressure was more on the president, who needed the Evangelical community's vote more than the bishop did. As he hung up the phone, he thought, "What can I do this time to win Beatrice back to my side and not lose my daughter, Monde?"

"Mr. President, your call?"

"Sure, Maicon, let's see what we can do with the Food Security Agency (FSA)."

The president and his Chief of Staff left the phone room and went into the operational room to address the FSA.

Meanwhile, on the other side of the country's capital, Bishop Mwendashi was deeply worried. She had protected the life of the father of the son she never had an opportunity to raise. But she was happy that her son had a caring father in Bwembya.

Another part of her did not want harm to come to her first love and father of her child. Even President Zeibous knew it and had been playing hardball to shield her from him. He excused it by saying, "Never fall again for that rebel provocateur; he means no good for you."

Coming out of her stupor, she rubbed her right eye with her left hand and called out to her driver and bodyguard, "Devon, come over here."

"Yes, ma'am."

"I am sorry I got mad at you."

"It's okay, ma'am."

"No, it wasn't. I shouldn't have. Again, sorry."

"Sure. Can I say something, ma'am?"

"Yes, say it."

"You're one of a kind, ma'am. I am just a nobody and you pay me very well. And you still say sorry to your servant."

"Come here, come," and Devon came. She hugged him and patted him on the back. The two drove off to the bishop's house.

TIMES OF ZAMBIA

"The Boss Has Escaped."

The nation's most notorious gang leader and godfather of dope has escaped from the most secure prison in Zambia, sources have revealed. There is utter chaos in the intelligence quarters, and the public is panicking and asking many questions. The Zeibous administration, which won its last presidential bid on a strong showing on law and order, has come under scrutiny as to why the notorious criminal and kingpin escaped under their watch...

It was the first news item in the nation's oldest newspaper. Other local and regional newspapers carried similar headlines.

For over 20 years, four successive governments had failed to apprehend "The Boss" and his "Arrogance Cartel."

The cartel had drug rings across the nation, organized on the structure of the government in power. Others even termed it the "shadow anti-government."

At the helm was The Boss, and his second in command was Fube Mutomboko, the mastermind of the Arrogance Cartel. Fube was recently reported deceased. After his death and in the absence of The Boss, it was speculated that The Boss's young son had assumed leadership. No one has any knowledge of who that son is.

Everyone in the nation wanted to find out The Boss's identity. When presidential candidates Willy Mzeche and Zeibous Mukangalume announced their campaigns, their promises included arresting The Boss "within 100 days in power." President

Zeibous Mukangalume received a landslide win with 71% of the vote. And after barely 89 days in power, The Boss was arrested and, after two years, found guilty and imprisoned.

His government could do nothing wrong after that. One commentator had written that, "Even when the president farts, he is adulated for adding an ounce of blessed gas to the atmosphere."

He had appointed the leader of the biggest Protestant ministry in the country, the Grand Complex and Cathedral, which he also attended regularly for mass and services, as his personal and government spiritual advisor. Bishop Mwendashi's church had skyrocketed to over 100,000 members after the appointment.

Recently, rumors have swelled that the president is either seeing the bishop or that they could even have had a child together.

Meanwhile, another rumor gaining traction was that Mr. Willy Mzeche had surged in the polls after the news of The Boss's escape, which sources closest to the presidency had confirmed caused President Zeibous Mukangalume much anxiety."

[9] PUBLIC PANIC

"Maicon, is my speech ready?"

"Yes, Your Excellency, I am told so."

Maicon Sibanzye quickly summoned Kalikeka Mumbi, the president's speechwriter, to the People's Office, as they called the presidential office. The two spent about 45 minutes working on the speech to be presented at the national music festival to be held at the Old Mulungushi International Convention Center in Lusaka.

Returning to the People's Office, the president motioned for Margarita Sondashi, the office secretary, to call Maicon back.

Within three minutes, Maicon knocked on the door.

"Come in, and please close the door behind you," the president instructed.

"Yes, Your Excellency," Maicon entered and closed the door.

"Did you make arrangements with Greyson Mushabati?"

"Yes, Your Excellency, but…"

"But what, Maicon?"

"Your Excellency, he wants K50 million now and another K50 million after the project."

"Okay, have you given it to him?"

"No, Your Excellency. I wanted to confirm with you first."

"Confirmed…and…"

"Your Excellency."

"No loose ends, you hear me. If anything goes wrong, you know what to do."

"Affirmative, Excellency."

Maicon left.

It was around 11:00 a.m., and the festival was scheduled to begin at 5:00 p.m.

Shortly after returning to the People's Office, Maicon met with the president again to report.

"All set, Your Excellency."

"Anything else?"

"There is, Sir. The fire will start on the second-floor balcony and make its way to the rear of the auditorium. By the time it reaches the VIP table, the Secret Service will have rescued you. Just in case something goes wrong, Sir, go under the table; it will protect you."

"Don't worry, they didn't call me Lightning for nothing during the freedom fighting days."

"I know, Your Excellency, it's just a precaution."

"Let's go!"

DIAMOND TV - BREAKING NEWS

"300 Plus Perish in Festival Fire," it was headlined.

"Three hundred and counting have been confirmed dead in a mysterious fire that broke out at the prestigious national festival," Diamond TV has learned.

The country was stunned, especially the families of those who had sent their children to perform at the 52nd National Musical Memorial (NMM). Each of the over five hundred participants had been sponsored by different stakeholders, and the winners were invited to participate in the regional musical competition featuring all eight neighboring countries.

Monde's close friend, Angela, was one of the participants. Angela had invested hours of practice and had told Monde, "I am delighted and honored to dedicate any trophy I might win to you, Sister." Monde and Angela had been friends since kindergarten, both raised by single mothers.

When Bishop Mwendashi's ministry began to take off, Angela's mother, Mebelline Katema, was one of the original choir members. When the previous long-serving reverend passed away, Mebelline and Pastor Mwendashi had recruited new members for the Mission Choir, which was later renamed the Grand Cathedral Choir (GCC). Angela was a member of GCC.

"Trust in God, dear sister; her soul must be in the bosom of Father Abraham according to scripture," Bishop Mwendashi, flanked by her daughter Monde, encouraged Mebelline over the phone.

As Mebelline continued to mourn, Monde added, "Mebelline, I want to be one of the pallbearers if you don't mind."

"No, I don't mind, Monde. Please escort your childhood friend into glory, just as she would have liked."

The three women hugged around the phone and mourned while watching the breaking news. An anchor then announced, "I interrupt the news to report that President Zeibous is now in stable condition. He had been critically injured in the fire at the festival where he was about to give an opening speech. ZIS has confirmed that the president's Chief of Staff, Mr. Maicon Sibanzye, has succumbed to smoke inhalation and is now dead, joining the over 350 deceased persons."

The nation was in mourning.

"Excuse me, my queen, I must make a call."

"Sure, Mother."

The bishop stepped forward, took out a small cellphone she only used occasionally, and dialed in absolute secrecy. The phone rang thrice and then stopped. There was no answer.

Not even the Secret Service to answer, Bishop Mwendashi thought.

Just then, she heard Monde calling, "Mother, he's speaking now, come!"

"Who's speaking?" the bishop asked as she ran downstairs to the living room to listen to the television.

"My countrymen and women, as you can see, I have just survived an assassination attempt, but I can't say the same for the 350-plus other innocent citizens," President Zeibous began, wrapped in bandages across half of his head.

"I am informing the nation that the arsonist has been gunned down and is now deceased. His name is Greyson Mushabati, a person known to our law enforcement officers. They found K50 million in his car, and his phone revealed that the last several calls he made were traced to The Boss. We believe, and our competent intelligence officers have confirmed, that it is the same Boss who recently escaped from prison and is the mastermind."

As she stood there listening to the televised speech, her limbs began to go numb. The phones she was holding fell to the floor. She removed her wig and collapsed onto the leather couch, looking dejected.

"Is everything okay, Mother?" Monde inquired as she picked up the scattered phone pieces and tended to her visibly rattled mother.

"No, not everything is fine, Monde…" Bishop Mwendashi passed out on the couch.

"Help, help, please someone help my mother!" Monde shouted.

She woke up around 4:38 a.m. Monde was leaning on her hospital bed, fast asleep. She was in a secluded ward at Vindondo

Medical Center (VMC). It was quiet and calm. She got out of bed easily and, without disturbing Monde, tiptoed to the washroom and back.

When she returned, Monde was awake.

"How do you feel, Mother?"

"I feel better. What happened to me?"

"You fainted, Mother. You scared all of us. I thought you were going to die, but…"

"Everything is going to be just fine," the bishop tenderly held Monde in her arms and massaged her voluminous brunette hair.

"You've grown into such a beautiful woman. You know I pray for you every day?"

"I know, Mother. I have been your pain all these years…"

"Don't say that. To the contrary, I wouldn't know what I would have done if it weren't for the Lord and for you, dear.

Everything I have and do is for you. Even my ministry is…"

"Mother, what are you talking about?"

"Yes, I must, dear. You just saw what happened; the Lord can call me home anytime."

"Shh, shh, Mother. Get back into bed and I will fetch a nurse to make a cup of coffee for you," Monde soothed her mother as she tucked her in methodically.

Then her phone rang. Monde reached into her mother's handbag, retrieved the phone, and answered it. It was the same phone that had been dropped and which she had reassembled.

It was now after sunrise, and a few of her servants and elders had come to visit her at VMC. They were all touched by her compassion when Monde told them her mother had fainted upon hearing about the fire's victims, including Monde's friend Angela. The word would later spread to the rest of the congregation that their bishop was truly anointed with a unique touch of compassion. Many families, including those who did not attend the Grand Cathedral, and the mayor of Lusaka, would later invite her to officiate at the state funeral for all those who had perished in the fire.

"Monde, please ask everyone to give me a moment alone; I would like to answer this call," she asked politely.

When everyone had left the room, she answered the phone.

"I heard what happened and I also saw your missed calls," the president began.

"Mhm…" the bishop responded in acknowledgment.

"How do you feel this morning?"

"I am better. I will be discharged soon. And yourself, how are you?"

"Don't worry. I was only brushed by the flames. My heart goes out to all who perished and their families. Maicon was killed in the fire too."

"Oh, I am so sorry."

"Me too. He was this nation's best Chief of Staff…"

"Don't despair, Mr. President; you will be blessed with another."

"We already did."

"How so?"

"The Cabinet decided. They wanted everything to look normal to encourage the public."

"Oh, I thought it was too early and some might find it strange."

"You're always looking at the big picture with a big heart. That's why everyone loves you, Beatrice."

"Everyone?"

"I mean, even me," the president chuckled.

"I know you, sneaky fox. But on a serious note…"

"How sure are we that it was Bwembya who killed those innocent souls? You wanted to ask, didn't you?"

"Yes. I think you need more time to investigate, as anyone can take advantage."

"I agree. But there was also a confession from Greyson and four other conspirators…"

"But I didn't hear those mentioned."

"Right. It's classified. But Beatrice, don't support that heartless liar; he's a killer, a monster. He wanted me dead and was not afraid to use innocent people as collateral. I heard that even my daughter's friend died!"

"Yeah, she was devastated, you should have seen. But you are to blame, too."

"B-u-t, b-but…" the president stammered. He was shaken and he started to perspire on the phone.

"I meant to say that, indirectly. You put him in a cell like a cornered rat. Do you expect that he would have a normal state of mind?"

With a sigh of relief, the president said, "I think you have a point, Beatrice."

"And here's my request, please do an investigation, give him due process. I would be more satisfied to see him pay for his crimes if evidence points to him."

"We will."

After the conversation, the president was bubbly as if a very heavy burden had been lifted off his shoulders.

"She didn't connect the dots but she almost did. I think I have won her sympathy," the president thought.

And just before he hanged up, Bishop Mwendashi inquired, "Hello, are you still there?"

"Oh, yes, Beatrice, did something else

come up?"

"No, Zeib, I just wanted to remind you to save my son."

"I promise. He'll be safe."

Bishop Mwendashi hanged up the phone.

***

The news of The Boss's escape sent shivers through the drug prevention wings of the government. President Zeibous set up a task force involving the Anti-Drug Commission (ADC), Anti-Corruption Commission (ACC), the Inspector General of Police (IG), and ZIS to conduct investigations into the arson and "come up with conclusive findings within three months." The task force was headed by Zebulun Kaichefya, a retired army general.

General Kaichefya did not waste time but became concerned when he saw a link nobody else had noticed during the investigation. He decided to meet with the president.

"Your Excellency, I asked to see you because of something that does not make sense to me."

"What is it, General Kaichefya?"

"Sir, I know that the late Mr. Maicon Sibanzye was your Chief of Staff…"

"What about him, General?" The president asked quickly.

"Sir, I have a video in which CCTV footage shows him handing an envelope to Mr. Greyson Mushabati, the same envelope found in Mr. Mushabati's car."

"Show me the video."

As the president watched, he saw his late Chief of Staff handing the same envelope to the very man accused of having links to the Arrogance Cartel.

"Son of a…I mean, this traitor, he…"

"Mr. President…"

"Yes, General?"

"You said something, Sir?"

"Oh, no, I was expressing my disappointment over my late Chief of Staff. What do you think of this video, General?"

"It's obvious, Sir, that someone from your office was working with the Arrogance Cartel."

"Yes, yes, I see that. So, what happens next?"

"Mr. President, you know the opposition will point fingers at you if this video is leaked."

"I agree. How many people know about this?"

"At the moment, only me and the young IT man who brought it to my attention."

"Good. General, what's the name of the young man?"

"He's John. I think John Daka. He's with ZIS."

"Alright, let's do this. Leave the video with me. I am quite busy at the moment; I will be meeting the new German ambassador to Zambia for accreditation. I will review it again tonight, and my office will contact you early tomorrow morning. Does this sound reasonable, General?"

"Yes, but…"

"But what, General?"

"Anyway, it's nothing, Your Excellency. I will be waiting tomorrow."

Everyone was tuned to the television that morning. The Zambia National Broadcasting Corporation (ZNBC), a government agency, had announced that the president would address the nation that morning. The whole country was attentive to ZNBC when the president spoke from State House via a teleprompter.

"My countrymen and women, our nation has faced challenges that have only sharpened our resolve for vigilance. Thanks to the machinations and savagery of the Arrogance Cartel, fear has gripped the young and old. But as your president, I will not rest until the culprits are brought to justice.

"That's why I instituted a task force to look into the arson that killed 502 people, including my Chief of Staff. I myself barely survived.

"Today, I bring you more bad news. I wish that I could have soothed your hearts in these perilous times, but sadly, I am unable to.

"General Kaichefya, our beloved Purple Order recipient and a national treasure, was found gunned to death in his home today. The killers left behind the Arrogance Cartel's signature symbol of a charred coat.

"Further, the entire family of a savvy and dependable civil servant in the Ministry of Information, Mr. John Daka, was massacred around 5:00 am today. Mr. Daka had joined the task force to provide the much-needed technical support, but today he, his wife, and his son were brutally murdered. The same charred coat was found at the murder scene. Mr. Daka was only 32 years of age.

> Today, like we did with the 502, I have declared that flags should fly at half-mast in all official buildings in honor of our deceased servants of the state.
> I, President and Commander-in-Chief of the Zambian armed forces, pledge today that I will hunt down the recluse Mumba Makayi Milando Bwembya, famously known as The Boss, and his Arrogance Cartel until two outcomes have taken place: either he is captured or killed. I have, thenceforth, signed an emergency presidential declaration—an executive order—to bring down the cartel and all its associates. Mr. Bwembya must be brought to me dead or alive.
> And to ensure that no other innocent member of this great country becomes a victim, I am appointing myself as chairman of the joint task force.

"The speech captivated the entire nation. However, people received the news with mixed feelings. Opposition leader

Yussouf Banda of the DPP issued a statement that read in part, 'We listened to the president's address with skepticism. If this matter was of grave concern, why didn't he hold a press conference so that the people could seek clarity? It all seems too convenient to be believed. We, the opposition DPP, will continue to seek clarity over this matter and continue to ask questions...'

"However, there was general consensus in the nation that President Zeibous's administration had taken the right step. The president's party, the Democratic National Alliance (DNA), looked poised to win with a landslide majority in the next elections slated to take place in less than one and a half years.

Within two months of active investigation following the president's speech, the joint task force established that, indeed, the Arrogance Cartel was responsible for the death of the 502 and the injury of over 1300 people at the music festival. They also confirmed that the cartel sponsored the assassination of General Kaichefya and John Daka and his family.

Just before the joint task force released its report, President Zeibous asked Bishop Mwendashi, the nation's Spiritual Advisor, to pray for the report and what would follow.

When Bishop Mwendashi met the president and all the members of the joint task force in the presidential chambers at State House, she was greatly troubled but tried not to show it.

Holding the president's hands, she prayed, "Father, give us the wisdom and speed to apprehend this notorious criminal before the nation begins to be jittery..." to which the president and his joint task force said, "Amen!"

But when she continued and said, "You, O Lord, put us in power and You can take us out..." the president and his task force went uncharacteristically silent.

From that moment, the manhunt officially began. A state of emergency had been declared that same day, meaning there was a curfew from 6:00 pm until 5:00 am each day until the elections were held.

But the order to arrest or kill The Boss saddened the bishop greatly.

[10] THE LIBRARY

"Mwanga, I have something to tell you," Monde said.

That morning, Mwanga had received a message from the Team that they were going with his father to the old hacienda in Mwinyilunga, in northwestern Zambia. Their initial plan of taking The Boss to hide at Kalene was foiled when they go intel that the Zambian army was spotted in the area.

"Rather than starting a war, I would prefer to spend a few days just enjoying nature," The Boss had mentioned.

So, they opted for Mwinyilunga hacienda instead. Mwanga was going to join them there as soon as he got a green light to go, he would fly in his family's chopper to the northwest. Because of the tension in the country owing to his father's escape from prison, he had wanted to spend some time with his girlfriend, Monde, at the Lusaka ranch. Monde was supposed to go to the ranch the previous week, but she had to attend Angela's funeral and then wait for another few more days to recuperate.

"Well, you can come over next Saturday, but I will have you stay until Sunday, is that okay?"

"Yes, Darling, and we attend church together on Sunday."

***

It was Sunday morning. Monde was still in her room when Chisanshi knocked on her door which she had left ajar.

"Come in," Monde was expecting Mwanga to show his face but it rather Chisanshi who entered.

Monde struggled to cover her tummy

which she had been admiring.

"I am so sorry, I thought it was your boss," Monde apologized.

"My apologies, too, ma'am. My Master says that you can meet him in the library."

"Sure. Tell him to give me fifteen or so minutes."

"Understood, ma'am," Chisanshi said, and left.

Monde thought for a moment, "He saw my tummy, but thank God he didn't see my boobs. I had pulled my blouse upwards, and they were covered."

Monde derived much comfort in that thought.

"Now, I must meet him for what might be the most consequential meeting of mine and his lifetime. "I must tell him today, I just feel it," she kept talking in her thoughts while selecting a matching sweater to go with her skirt outfit. She chose a brown sweater and walked thoughtfully downstairs into the library.

When she was nearing the place, there was a large double door rim that only opened with the push of a button. She stopped there momentarily, and before she could push the button, the started to open on its own. She followed the door as it ushered her into a seemingly empty space. There were a few books on the shelf, but not many enough to earn the room the name library.

"But why is everyone calling it the library?" Monde thought.

Then three doors opened, and she Mwanga tease, "If you can guess where I am, you can ask me for anything today?"

"Are you really sure?"

"Yes, I am."

"For anything?"

"Anything."

She was, in fact, gauging the sound vibrations as she asked him questions. She went for the door that was to her far left. It was the room.

"I got you," she jumped on him and kissed him.

Mwanga took Monde's right hand and gently caressed it. He brought her closer to his chest and held her tightly there.

Like a little girl she blushed and closed her eyes. Then she reminded him that she had guessed right and she was ready to name her prize. Mwanga agreed by nodding his head up and down.

"Okay, what I want is to tell you something, and you can't get mad, mhm?"

Again, Mwanga nodded in agreement.

"I am pregnant," she said, looking away from him while pretending to be flipping the pages of a book.

"Wha-t, pre…wha-t…" Mwanga was stunned.

"Yes, you heard me right, and it's…" "Darling, that's the best news I have ever heard in my entire life," Mwanga shouted while kissing Monde nonstop.

"…yours," she finally uttered the word Mwanga had inhibited because of kissing her.

"I know," he said, and continued to embrace her tightly wrapping himself around her chest.

Monde felt so loved and relieved. She closed her eyes and relaxed her mind and muscles. Mwanga could hear soft, teary sounds coming from Monde. "Thank you, Jesus. He accepted without a fight. Thank you, Jesus. He accepted us!"

"Of course, I accept. You bled when we did it the first time. I knew that you were a…"

"…virgin, yes. But I was still afraid that you would…"

"What, doubt you? No, Darling. Even if it was from another man, I would still have you both!"

"Really?" Monde began to cry.

"Stop it, stop crying, Darling."

"They are tears of joy, Mwanga. Right now, I would do anything for this feeling. I know that ahead of me there will be shame, disappointment, and pain. People will curse me and my mom and…"

"Stop that, my love. I'll always be there for you; doesn't that matter at all?"

"Yes, it does, it matters a million times more. I better enjoy this moment."

The couple embraced each other and remained in each other's arms for close to an hour. Monde fell asleep still holding onto Mwanga, her tears unwiped.

As they kissed, three bodyguards were busily ushering a prominent figure into the library. The duo was in the middle of their kiss when a rough voice greeted her:

"How are you, young lady?"

When she opened her eyes, it was The Boss.

"I know you, The Boss! I saw you on TV when you were arrested. What are you doing here?" Monde exclaimed, quickly rearranging her pink bra which she had dropped during the kiss.

"Yes, it's me, and also your boyfriend's father."

Monde was startled. She looked disappointedly at Mwanga, her gestures speaking volumes as words failed her.

"I know, Love, my apologies, but I had to do it for Dad."

Mwanga held Monde tight and tried to console her.

Then Matafwali Kalonji, the Concordia Killer, said, "Your boyfriend's dad wants to borrow you for a few days till we figure out what to do next."

"You mean kidnapping me," Monde screamed.

"Mmh…well…mhm…we prefer you keeping us company to kidnapping you, in fact," Matafwali answered.

" I haven't even had time to thank you, Son, for Operation 7:59. I'm told it was divinely inspired by Buggie's church?"

Everyone present looked at each other with surprise. No one had any clue who "Buggie" was, including Monde, The Boss's captive.

"Thanks, Dad, but I don't attend Buggie's church; I go to the Grand Cathedral under Bishop Mwendashi," Mwanga corrected.

Matafwali Kalonji began to laugh. He laughed so hard that he fell off his seat.

When he composed himself, he was about to say something, but when he looked in The Boss's direction, he abruptly stopped.

Everyone, including Monde, saw that awkward moment.

To reignite the sense of excitement and joy that had existed before Matafwali's antics, The Boss cracked a joke.

"You see, guys," he began, "Matafwali almost gave me a heart attack when I first recruited him. I began to notice that my toothpicks were getting fewer and fewer. I called all my employees and inquired if anyone among them was stealing them. Everyone said no, including Matafwali. But then, to look innocent, he said, 'Boss, it's surely not me, because each time I use one, I put it back in the same bottle!'"

Everyone—the team members, servants attending to The Boss, Mwanga, and Monde—began laughing uncontrollably. The only one who was not laughing was Matafwali.

It seemed by all measures that the joke served as a cathartic gesture. Even Monde, who had been tense and quiet as a benevolent captive, loosened up and asked a servant for "cold lemonade with some chocolate cookies."

When everybody was jovial and it started to feel normal despite the ongoing manhunt for the Arrogance Cartel, the conversation in the library became family-like with more jokes and teasing.

Mwanga seemed to be the most excited among them all, which caught his father's attention.

"Son, I'm sure you did us all proud, but aren't you a bit too excited?"

"Yes, Dad, but for another reason. You are going to be…"

Monde stood up quickly and tried to stop Mwanga from completing his sentence, but she was too late.

Mwanga ended with, "…a grandpa."

"What do you mean?" The Boss asked.

Monde stood between the father and his son and answered for Mwanga, "What he meant was that, as a result of the manhunt, you will now be elevated from Godfather to Grandfather."

Monde was looking at Mwanga while nodding her "yes, yes," but Mwanga didn't get it.

"Step aside, sweetheart. Let Mwanga respond. Everyone here can tell that he meant what he said; maybe you are just learning to know him," The Boss said to Monde.

Monde sat down rather dejectedly. She was furious that The Boss had held her captive and did not want to be associated with either Mwanga or The Boss, or the entire "crooked Arrogance Cartel," as she referred to it.

"My love…" Mwanga began to say something.

"Don't call me that. I am no longer your lover," Monde interrupted Mwanga.

"But anyway, as I started saying, Monde, I can't lie to my father. Father, Monde is pregnant with our child. Yes, you will be a real grandpa."

Members of the team and all the servants present applauded with loud cheers of "CONGRATULATIONS!"

But The Boss and Matafwali remained as silent as death. Shortly thereafter, everyone went coldly silent. Something was wrong; even Monde could sense it.

Mwanga was disturbed and turned to his father, asking, "I thought you would be very happy. Remember what we discussed at my eighteenth birthday?"

"I know, Son, and I should be the happiest here, and I am."

But before Mwanga could ask another question, The Boss asked everyone to leave the library, "except for my son, Matafwali, and you, Monde." It was the first time The

Boss had referred to Monde by her name since the encounter, and she felt that there was something more serious than a mere kidnapping at play.

Everyone left the library. Only The Boss, Mwanga, Monde, and Matafwali remained.

Looking intently at Mwanga, The Boss said, "I am happy for you, Son, and also sad. And more importantly, I am sorry."

"Why are you sorry, Dad? I thought this would cheer you up."

"Indeed, and you are very right, if it were under normal circumstances."

"But, Dad, our situation has always been like this, but we survive. Even this manhunt, I know, is the work of that schemer of a president. We shall cut off his head sooner rather than later…"

"End right there, Son. Matafwali, tell these two the truth."

"B-o-s-s, b-but…" Matafwali hesitated, "…everything?"

"I said everything. It's an order!"

Matafwali paused momentarily. Mwanga and Monde came close and reluctantly held each other's hands, ready to listen.

"Mwanga, Monde, what I am about to tell you may be very disturbing. My Boss kept it a secret from you, Mwanga, because he wanted to protect you, especially your heart."

"Just say it. I am not a child anymore. I am now going to be…"

"…22. Just go ahead," Monde urged.

Matafwali chuckled, cleared his throat, and said, "You two are biologically sister and brother…"

Mwanga and Monde jumped, letting go of each other's hands and gazing at each other spookily.

"No way!" Monde exclaimed.

"But how can that be?" Mwanga asked Matafwali, calmly and respectfully.

"Let me explain," Matafwali started, looking sympathetically towards The Boss, who had just dropped a tear for the first time in the more than eighteen years he had served him.

"Monde, your mother and The Boss were childhood sweethearts. Your maternal grandmother separated them just when Mwanga was conceived. Shortly after, your grandmother asked President Zeibous to marry your mother, and the result was you…"

Before Matafwali could continue, Monde collapsed and fainted. The new senior resident doctor, Dr. Phiri, was called in, as every senior staff member from the Kalene Hacienda had been transferred to the Lusaka Ranch because of the manhunt. Only a handful of men and women had been left on the Kalene and Mwinyilunga ranches.

"Dr. Phiri, how is Monde doing?"

"She's fine and the baby is fine and healthy, Son."

It was Dr. Phiri, twenty-one and a half years ago, who helped Beatrice, Mwanga's mother, to deliver Mwanga, at gunpoint. After kidnapping Dr. Phiri, his wife, Yuen, also a medical doctor, had divorced him and remarried. Their two sons, Mavimbo and Vozansa, were reclaimed by Dr. Phiri with the help of the Arrogance Cartel. Mavimbo was sent to China to train in guerrilla tactics. He was responsible for training the Arrogance Cartel in infiltration techniques. He was killed by a rival gang in Angola when a drug deal went bad.

Vozansa decided to follow in his father's footsteps. The Arrogance Cartel sponsored him to study medicine in Russia. He married there and stayed there.

When Mwanga was born, Mavimbo Phiri and Vozansa Phiri were in their early teens, and Dr. Phiri (who became known as Dr. Phiri Sr. after Vozansa became a medical doctor) had taken care of Baby Mwanga since then. Dr. Phiri Sr. regarded Mwanga as his own, a gesture that The

Boss had acknowledged during Mwanga's sixteenth birthday when he introduced him as "Mwanga's resident father."

On Dr. Phiri Sr.'s sixtieth birthday, Mwanga reciprocated. He gave him a bulletproof Bentley with a note that read, "To a deserved father who has been there for me since birth and truly loves me."

That statement and gesture summed up what had been the relationship between Mwanga and Dr. Phiri Sr. When Mwanga was sick, beaten by a wasp, had his circumcision, had his first ejaculation, or was celebrating a milestone, The Boss would say to Dr. Phiri Sr., "stand in for me." The bond between Mwanga and Dr. Phiri Sr. was even stronger than the one Dr. Phiri Sr. had with his own blood children.

"Do you think that our child would be cursed, Dr. Phiri?" Mwanga asked.

"I don't think so. Do you want her to abort?"

"No, Dr. Phiri. Even if I was pointed at with a gun, I wouldn't do that."

"Why, for religious or legal reasons?"

"For neither, Dr. Phiri. It is the fault of our parents, not ours."

"Good answer. Let's see what Monde says."

"Well, sure. And…"

"Hmh…I am listening, Son."

"Can I talk to Monde?"

"She's still mad and sad. Give her one or two more days. You don't want to exacerbate her blood pressure due to stress; it could affect the baby."

"Sure, sir. Anything for the baby and the mother," Mwanga conceded.

It was the most heated conversation the president and the bishop had ever had. It began with hyperboles and innuendos, avoiding their inner staffers. But then it became known to all their inner circles, with both warning their staffers not to disclose whatever was discussed to anyone "or there will be consequences," President Zeibous told his presidential staff.

"I told you to tread cautiously with Mila, didn't I, Mukangalume, mm, didn't I?"

"Beatrice..."

"Don't even call my name. You call yourself a man of the people, but the person who matters most to you, your own daughter, is just a phantom. Now, you even got her kidnapped because of your insatiable appetite for power!"

"Bishop, I am truly sorry. I am also very hurt. I am angry, just calm down..."

"Calm down, calm down. This is now the twenty-eighth day, and there's no sign of Monde...."

"I know, Bishop. We have now contracted Interpol to engage in the manhunt..."

"But have you told them that your own daughter is also missing, have you?"

The president did not answer. He, rather, gave an excuse that he was entering a policy meeting with his Council of Ministers, which included the Cabinet, deputy ministers, and permanent secretaries.

But the die was cast. Rumors at both the State House and the Grand Cathedral had started spreading that the president had a kidnapped daughter, and Monde could be the one.

To make it even more suspicious, Bishop Mwendashi's message that Sunday was entitled, "Search Carefully." Quoting Luke 15:8-10, she read during her televised broadcast, "Or what woman, having ten silver coins, if she loses one, does not light a lamp, sweep the house, and SEARCH CAREFULLY until she finds it? And when she finds it, she calls her friends and neighbors together, saying, 'Rejoice with me, for I have found the PIECE which I lost.'"

At first, many of her followers thought that she had preached that sermon to comfort the nation. But as the rivalry between her and the president began to grow, many people revisited her sermon. A review that began on Movie TV went viral.

Misheck Mpolombo, a Movie TV senior national commentator, said, "Did you listen to the bishop's sermon? It was being addressed to only one person in the country, the president. Remember, she mentioned a woman who lost a coin (child) and implored the president to 'search carefully,' telling him that a 'piece' of her was lost." The commentary was trending on Facebook, X, and TikTok. People were talking about it for three weeks consecutively.

Bishop Mwendashi refused to do interviews on that topic and took three weeks off from work. During those three weeks, she joined some church members to search for Monde. She was particularly enraged when, each time the president gave updates to the nation, he wanted to garner support for his reelection campaign and did not mention the people affected, especially her daughter, Monde, who had been missing for close to four months. In private, the president had given an order to "find Monde Mwendashi at all costs," but no official injunction was issued.

It was Mebelline who first suggested to her best friend and sister-in-Christ, Bishop Mwendashi, that Monde could have been kidnapped by Boss Boy.

"Sister, I may have something that could help."

"What is it, Mebelline?"

"I remember my late daughter, my Angela, now an angel as her name is, telling me something about Monde."

"What did she say?"

"She revealed that Monde had fallen in love with a rough boy at school whom they called…"

"Boss Boy…" the bishop completed her sentence.

"So, you know?"

"Monde herself told me. You know we don't hide anything from each other."

"That's truly comforting because I had almost begun to think that I betrayed you."

"No, you didn't, but you have given me a good idea. I should find out more about this boy."

"Sure, meanwhile, let's have a cup of tea together before we attend the prayer meeting tonight."

"Indeed."

"Beatrice, I have some urgent news," President Zeibous announced.

"Remember I told you not to call me unless you had good news about Monde?" the bishop challenged the president.

"Yes, it's about Monde, but I…"

"What, did they find her? Is she okay…?"

"Rest assured they may be close. The news is that Boss Boy is actually Bwembya's son..."

"It's a gimmick, right? You're trying my patience. Is this another tactic to hush me off? I don't agree. My daughter can't be going out with her own brother. Do you hear how that even sounds? Do you?"

Bishop Mwendashi's preexisting condition reemerged. She lapsed while she was on the secure line with the president.

"Beatrice...Beatrice...Beatrice..." the president wanted to know what was happening to the bishop. There was no response. The president tried to call again, and there was still no response.

After a short while, Devon received a call from an "unknown" caller. He picked it up.

"It's me, President Zeibous..."

"You could even be the Pope, but as a good Catholic turned Pentecostal, I would not believe..."

"Devon, please don't let us argue. It could be an emergency. Please check on your boss. I think she has fainted…"

Devon did not wait another minute. He dropped his phone and rushed back to the Lexus SUV he had left to give his boss privacy. When he arrived, it was true that his boss had fainted on the steering wheel. He managed to resuscitate her, then he went back to get his phone where he had dropped it. To his surprise, the president was still on the line.

"How is she?"

"Mr. President, I am so sorry for not believing you…"

"Skip the formality and apologies. How is she?"

"I managed to make her recoup. You were very right, sir."

Devon could not believe that he had just talked to the President of Zambia.

He knows my name. He has my number.
Wow, I am so important, Devon thought.

Back at the vehicle, he found his boss talking to the president on a secure line. The conversation went on for about an hour, and he could see that his boss was not happy. She kept lifting her right hand while holding her "other" phone with her left hand.

"The conversation cannot be constructive," he thought.

Just then, he could see his boss looking in his direction and beckoning him with her left phone-holding hand to return to the vehicle.

He did.

"Hello here," a police officer knocked.

"Please hold, I am coming," a female voice said.

When she opened the door, Melody could see at least seven police officers. Two were standing in front of her at the door, and the rest were already trying to peek through the windows of the house and the horse stables.

"Who lives here?" one police officer asked.

"Me and my family," Melody answered.

"Can we see your registration card?"

"Sure, give me a minute to retrieve it."

Melody returned with her "reg," and it read:

Melody Chanda, born on March 15, 1971, in Chambishi Township, Copperbelt Province, village Mushinge, Chief Mwendapole, Northern Province.

"That's what we have on our registry," the second officer confirmed.

"If I may ask, officers, is anything the matter?"

The officers first conversed among themselves, and after a show of nodding heads, one of them said, "Nothing serious... by the way, we are wondering if you have seen this man?"

The officer showed a photo to Melody. It was the picture of Mwanga. Looking intently at the officers, Melody said, "No. I have no idea."

The officers left.

[12] THE ELECTION

"Melody, I want to talk to your boss," Monde demanded. "Sure, but which one?" "You know the one I mean," Monde pointed at her belly. "Right away," Melody departed.

Mwanga was waiting to be summoned in the room. The room was next to a den separated by a curtain. Those in the den could not see those in the room, but those in the room could see those in the den.

Mwanga paced the den from one end to the other. She could see that he was tired, but she seemed to be enjoying it. She giggled and then put her two hands on her mouth and whispered to her growing baby in her tummy, "See, look, that's your father or uncle. It's up to you. By the way, I love him because he's the first person to love me for who I am and to give me a child and a brother I have longed for all my life."

Monde laughed, albeit silently. Meanwhile, Mwanga, who had waited for almost an hour in the den to be called in, fell asleep on the couch.

"Come in," Monde invited.

But there was no response.

She called again, "Boss Boy, come in and greet your junior."

But again, there was no response. So, she walked toward the den, opened the curtain, and found Mwanga fast asleep. She slowly walked towards him and sat right next to him, beginning to stroke his hair. She took out his cell phone, placed his thumb on the screen, and opened the phone. She took a selfie with him, and she was about to send it to her trusted boyfriend, Gertrude, when Mwanga woke up.

"Hey, hi sleepyhead," she greeted him.

"Does that mean you've forgiven me, not mad at me?" Mwanga asked, yawning unceremoniously.

"I was not mad at you, Pumpkin. I was angry with myself, my mother, your father, and the president."

"Yeah, why they kept such important information from us is unfathomable to me."

"To me, too, Boss Boy."

"Hey, Darling, tell me you didn't use my phone to contact someone outside?"

"No. Actually, I wanted to but..."

"But what?"

"But then you woke up. See..." Monde grabbed the phone from him and showed him the message she had composed and instructed *AI* to send later.

"Thanks for not sending..."

"But why? You sound concerned."

"Well, it's because…"

"Of what? You are afraid to be arrested? Me, too. Now, I hate Zeibous more than I love your father."

"Really?"

"Yes."

"But why, aren't you mad about what we have done?"

"No. Not anymore. Thinking about it, I know that my mother has never stopped loving your dad. Do you know how many times Zeibous has tried to kill your dad but for my mom?"

"Really?"

"Yes. I used to think it was because she was a pastor and believed in the good of all humans. But after what I now know, it is obviously because your dad was her first love and she's never forgotten him."

"I see. Darling, I have something else to tell you."

The manner in which Mwanga said it made Monde very worried. She held him by his sleeves and begged him to tell her the truth.

"Sure, it's about Mom, I mean, your mother."

"And about her?"

"We have kidnapped her, too…"

"But why? Was I not an adequate ransom? You know my mother will preach this Sunday!" Monde was irate. She began to hit Mwanga on the head with a couch pillow.

"We're not going to keep her for long. In fact, we just wanted her to know what we unearthed."

"What is it? I mean, what did you discover? Please tell me, Mwanga. Remember, she's also your mother?"

"I know. Dad has instructed that no single hair on her head will be harmed. Know that Dad always keeps his promises."

"Mila, why after all these years, why cause mischief now? I should be mad at you, but, surprise, I am not," Bishop Mwendashi addressed her captor, The Boss.

"You know that you are not my captive…"

"So, I can leave right now?"

"Of course, but first I want you to meet your daughter, Monde…"

"I knew it; I suspected that you were holding her."

"Really, does your ex-husband also know that I have his daughter?"

"He suspects that, no leads yet."

"Is she safe?"

"Yeah, recently, she's expressed a desire not to return. She…"

"No, Mila. I think you are manipulating her. You're brainwashing her."

"Anyway, you will be meeting her soon. And…"

"And what… that she is going out with her brother? How can you allow that, surely, Mila? Do you even fear God?"

"It's not like you think, Buggie. You will hear the truth… let's go."

Mwanga, Monde, and Matafwali were already seated in the library. Monde was browsing through some "Family" magazines while sipping her favorite lemonade. Mwanga and Matafwali were playing in solo, and they were loud and focused.

Then the door opened.

He stood up like a pole, his eyes falling on her face. She just gave one glance, and no one could have anticipated what happened next.

She flew like a kite, and he stood there like a statue. She hugged him, kissed him, inspected him, and cleaned the dirt on him that he didn't have. She laughed, cried, smiled, smirked, frowned, and mourned all at the same time.

Mwanga began to cry like an unstoppable baby.

Bishop Mwendashi didn't know what to do with her long-lost son.

Everyone was stunned. No one uttered a word. They simply sat there watching as scene after scene played out in front of them.

The first one to be affected was Monde. She rushed to hug the two, crying like a little child.

Then it was The Boss. He walked towards the three, majestic and steady, and he also joined in to hug the three. He was in tears, although no sound came from him.

For Matafwali, it was more for his boss than for the other three. That was the second time he had seen his boss cry. The first time was about six months prior when he learned that Monde was pregnant with his son's child. They were tears of mixed emotions - joy because he would be a grandfather. However, sad because it was between two step-siblings. The Boss blamed himself for everything.

Then they sat there. Bishop Mwendashi was not leaving Mwanga alone. She just kept admiring how handsome he had grown to be. She remembered giving birth to him and nothing else. And he was right in her arms. She was beside herself with joy.

"I wanted very much to be there when you were…"

"Yes, I came to the Grand Cathedral."

"That, I had no idea."

"Oh, Bishop, I learned just recently that you were my mother. But I surely was enjoying your sermons."

"Please, call me 'mother,' if you don't mind!"

"I enjoyed listening to you, Bishop, I mean, Mother."

"You mean, you listen to my messages?"

"Yes. I even came or was coming to church before all these…"

"Oh, my sweet boy, so you heard me preach?"

"Every Sunday for almost seven months. At first, it was to win Monde, then…"

"Then you preached about gaining the whole world or something…"

"And losing your soul…"

"Mhm… that one… I never slept for the entire week. So…"

"Yes, so what happened?"

"I attended church the following Sunday, and when you asked to pray after you…"

"In a sinner's prayer, I did."

"Oh my God, you were born again. My son is a child of the Most-High God."

Then Bishop Mwendashi went into praise. She thanked God for His goodness and for making her meet her son.

This is just too nice a moment to disturb, The Boss thought.

Then, he beckoned to Matafwali to follow him, and when he was leaving, he whispered into Monde's ear to let Mwanga and his mother know that the discussions had been postponed to the next day.

The two left the library.

***

"Um…where do I start?" The Boss said, gently clearing his throat.

The five sat in the library, ready for a serious conversation. The library itself was located in the basement. It was equipped with military hardware and software and could double as a bunker in times of war or conflict. Its radio transmission systems could detect any sophisticated weapons and alert the enemy. It also had a complex exit track that led to an underground tunnel.

"We're all ears, Mila. Are you going to let me go today as you promised?" Bishop Mwendashi asked The Boss.

"Of course, listen and be strong because of what I am going to say.

"What is it…Mila?" the bishop sifted through a plethora of emotions building up within her mind.

"Monde is *with* child, and Mwanga *is* the father…"

All went silent. The atmosphere changed; it became nebulous.

History can't be repeating itself, the bishop thought.

"What? Say… say that again," the shocked bishop said.

Matafwali quickly moved closer to the bishop and provided her with some napkins.

"*Here*, ma'am," Matafwali said.

The bishop accepted the offer and thanked Matafwali.

Meanwhile, Matafwali stayed there patiently until the bishop found herself again.

"The *kids* have decided that they are going to keep the child. I have expressed my apologies to them for being a bad parent…"

Bishop Mwendashi did not wait for The Boss to complete his sentence.

"But…Mila, that's unbelievable. You're taking the blame for *these* children's incestuous behavior. Don't you know that they can invite a curse not only on the unborn child but also on their lineage? In the Old Testament, it is written…"

The Boss interrupted his ex-girlfriend.

"Keep your religious nonsense away from here, Buggie. You're a bishop. You should at least link their behavior to your lack of informing Monde that she had a brother."

"And you, yourself, Mila, did *you* tell my son here that he had a sister? Isn't it *you* that prevented me from accessing my own son?" Bishop Mwendashi was enraged.

And then she went into deep thoughts, *When Monde introduced him to me, something was telling me that we were connected somehow, Oh, Lord, how did I miss the sign then, why didn't I know then that he was my son, it could have prevented all this?*

Seeing that their parents' quarrel was leading nowhere, Mwanga took Monde by her left hand and the two left the library.

Meanwhile, Bishop Mwendashi and The Boss continued to play the blame game until Matafwali intervened.

"I see that you are going nowhere by blaming each other. Why don't we postpone this meeting again until tomorrow?"

The suggestion seemed to please both sides, and they each returned to their bedrooms.

The next day was a Wednesday. Bishop Mwendashi was expected to lead the midday service. She would preach remotely, feigning to be on an emergency vacation to recover from the unconfirmed loss of her daughter, Monde.

Bishop Mwendashi had been preaching in the midweek service through a series entitled "Hope Does Not Disappoint." As she prepared for the teaching, she came to the passage of scripture where the Bible said, "If you don't *forgive* others their sins, your Heavenly Father will not *forgive* your sins, either." She paused there for a long time, meditating.

Then she walked up to The Boss' room, knocked on the door gently, and waited to be invited in.

"Who's that?" The Boss asked.

"Oh, it's *me*, Beatrice."

"Buggie, come in."

When she entered his room, The Boss was in his underwear. Looking the other way, she said, "Sorry, I didn't mean to intrude."

"What do you mean by intruding? Even if you presented yourself to me naked, I wouldn't manage you, anyway."

"What are you talking about, Mila?"

"You want to know the truth, Buggie? After you, I have never had the pleasure to enjoy another woman."

"What, all *these* years, but why?"

"Well, you think I am bluffing? Look at *it*..."

The Boss quickly dropped his underwear. At first, the bishop looked away, but then she couldn't resist watching what she saw.

"What, Mila, you got rid of *it*?" The bishop was shocked.

"For you, of course…now you believe me? I gave up on love after you to devote myself to the dream. But in reality… don't mind."

"Come on, go ahead and say it, come do," the bishop challenged The Boss, drawing closer and closer to him.

"You are the only woman I ever loved, Buggie. Period."

Just as he finished talking, her lips were already on his, and the two were kissing. When they ended the kiss, they stayed right there in each other's arms; they said nothing.

"Mh… um… I'm sorry, Mila. I…"

"Shh, I should be the one apologizing…"

"I disagree, it's me…"

As they tried to outdo one another, The Boss said, "I thought that because of being castrated, I wouldn't feel anything for a woman, and it's been true all these years, but with you everything just popped up. Isn't it amazing?"

"Surely, I am flattered, I mean it. But I also have a confession to make. I think about *you* from time to time…"

"'From time to time?'"

"Okay…at least every other day…" The bishop blushed.

"And then you cast me away to prison?"

"No, Mila, it's Zeib, Mila…" The bishop tried to explain. She moved closer to The Boss and hugged me, and then continued talking.

"He made me try to hate you so much. But the truth is, even when Mother forced me to marry him, we only did *it* two or three times, and I conceived. You know that we *divorced* immediately I gave birth..."

"You mean broke the engagement, Buggie?"

"Whatever, Mila – truth is, I have never loved anyone, too..."

"Apart from me, you mean, Buggie?"

"That's the absolute truth, my dear Mila..."

"...what about after that? Sorry for interrupting."

"Till now, God is my witness. And I was shocked that I remembered how to kiss *only* with you."

"Me, too, Buggie."

Then The Boss remembered.

"There's something I wanted to show you before you go, Buggie."

"What is it, Mila?"

"Matafwali, call in the Team," The Boss commented.

Before Matafwali returned, the bishop wanted to know what happened to that "boy who used to bring me small love notes in broken English from you when we were dating." The Boss paused, then he said that "Fube is the boy, but he died as a *real* man. I trusted that man like I trust my own heart. He served me till his last breathe." Bishop Mwendashi was sorry, and she cleared a tear that was rolling down The Boss' cheek.

Within minutes, the library was swarmed with people and turned into a studio. The large screen overlayed the room from wall to wall and everything was meticulously presented.

As the presentation began to roll in, Bishop Mwendashi was getting restless and jittery. As the film rolled halfway, the

bishop shouted, "I have seen enough!" And
she began to cry.

Monde and her mother drew closer to
each other and continued to cry in each
other's arms.

"Oh, poor Angela, my best friend. I
thought it was the Arrogance Cartel that
killed you when it turns out to be the
president," Monde sobbed inconsolably.

"And poor General John Daka, not to
mention the over 600 that died. Zeibous is
the devil incarnate," regretted the bishop.

Matafwali took time to explain to the
bishop that it had been the president's plan
all along to murder innocent Zambians and
then boost his reelection chances. He knew
that the atmosphere in the country was
tense owing to The Boss' escape, and he
pinned the blame for the fire at the
Mungungushi musical festival on the
Arrogance Cartel.

"And it has worked based on the most
recent polls. He'll win the reelection with a
landslide," informed The Boss.

"But aren't you going to stop him?" the bishop asked.

"Not now. We must let him win," Dorothy said.

"But why? You know that he's hoodwinked the nation," replied the bishop.

At that point, The Boss chimed in and gave the rationale.

"We will pretend that we know nothing so he can win. Meanwhile, we'll keep Monde here until she gives birth. She's already seven months pregnant; so, it won't be long…"

"But if he wins with a landslide, he'll be very powerful and he'll have command of both the State House and Parliament," the bishop commented.

"That's surely true. But remember that by then both Monde and your ministry will not suffer shame. In addition, *the higher you go…*"

"… *the harder the fall*," echoed Bishop Mwendashi, completing The Boss' thinking.

[13] SECOND TERM

The PPD came out a distant second place, giving the DNA a landslide victory with 71% of the total presidential vote in the national election. However, the opposition party, the New Generation Congress (NGC) led by Kaitano Chanda and comprising mainly the X, Y, and Z generations, scooped about 41% of the parliamentary seats. Under the system introduced by the previous PPD government, the NGC had become the new official opposition in parliament.

"What does this mean, Mother? I mean, the relationship between the PPD and the NGC?" Monde, who had just delivered a bouncy baby boy named Bwembya Mwendashi, asked.

"Mm...from what Zeibous explained, it means that the PPD gets to provide a president, but the NGC gets to lead the House. It's confusing, I know. And may I ask, what's this sudden interest in politics, Daughter?"

"Hmh...and why this sudden change of address from 'queen' to 'daughter,'" Monde joked.

"I asked you first, answer me, then I might answer you," teased the mother.

"You know, Mother, that the delivery process can change so many things about someone. With what is happening, I am seriously considering joining politics. I can't leave the governance of this great country to corrupt people and murderers anymore. I want to secure a reasonable future for my son," Monde revealed.

"Oh, whoa, that was unexpected. I should reverse my address; I think I should prefer 'daughter-queen' to 'queen'* only, going forward," the mother decided.

"If that's the case, be decisive and have tenacity like Esther…" Monde cut her mother off mid-sentence and said, "Esther never ruled; she only supported. I want to rule this country. I want to be like King David."

The mother did not say another word, she only nodded, and thought to herself, "What have I done to this girl."

"Look, they have neglected you. No one has come to see you since the attempted escape, and your Patron's arrest is imminent after the presidential landslide…"

"Officer…um…see, you're wasting your time. I'm not going to tell you anything. You've violated my prisoner rights by torturing me constantly for over six months…"

"You'll die here, you'll rot in this prison…"

"Spare yourself the trouble, I am afraid I am already dead; I died when I signed up to join The Boss years ago…"

Benjamin "Shokashoka" remained in solitary confinement at Chimbokaila Prison. President Zeibous and the disbanded joint task force had done everything they could to capture The Boss before the election but failed. After the election, they had gathered vital intel that the Arrogance Cartel had planned to "spill the beans, and that will put the Zeibous government to permanent shame."

"I am a lame duck, Jason. I must find Bwembya before he destroys me," the president confided in his new Chief of Staff and political adviser, Jason Mundiyah.

Jason came to prominence when he went on national television and defended the president's integrity.

"As a long-serving civil servant, both in the Hakainde and Hichilema administrations, I have never seen a leader as determined, committed to principle, and selfless as President Mukangalume…"

Then Jason did the unthinkable. When a rumor had begun to fester that the president had a child with Bishop Mwendashi, Jason appeared before a crowd of protesters and claimed he would be killed if the people did not believe that his deceased brother was Monde's father. He volunteered to provide DNA to prove his statement.

Several media houses took saliva from Jason, and it confirmed that he was distantly related to Monde, and the rumors came to an end.

When he was interrogated by the president himself about how his DNA ended up confirming a partial relationship to Monde, he lied that his paternal grandmother and the mother were step-sisters. Since then, the trust between Jason and the president was unbreakable.

"If you can sacrifice for me with your life, you can take a bullet for me. When I win reelection, you shall be my Chief of Staff," the president had promised.

He had kept his word.

"But, Mr. President, momentum is on your side. Your approval rating is the highest of any president since Zambian independence…"

"I am aware, Jason, but fortunately, I also know how Bwembya behaves…he can't be quiet for this long unless he's planning something major…honestly, the silence is killing me. I must move fast…"

Just when the president and his political advisor were talking, there was a knock on the People's Office, and it was the first secretary. She came to remind the president that his old friend, Moses Lwikisha, had been waiting for him. The president had asked for him when all options to catch The Boss had failed.

When they met, it was déjà vu all over again.

"Welcome to State House, my old friend. How have you been?"

"Thank you, Your Excellency. Without the gift you recently sent me, I would have been counting my marbles to my grave," the retired savvy intelligence tactician and the Mother's most accomplished "destroyer" said.

There was the usual exchange of pleasantries and a snack, and after that, they came to the reason the Destroyer was invited to the State House.

"Your take, Destroyer, as Jason explained, we have done what we should. What's your opinion?"

"Times have evolved, but the 'Masterpiece' is still using the old, rustic, and proven classics," the Destroyer said.

President Zeibous was taken aback when he heard the word "Masterpiece." Indeed, Bwembya had been famously known for his methodical and meticulous surgery-like missions. He was perfect in his intelligence and espionage role. The Mother herself gave him the name Masterpiece.

"I was given the name Mastermind, and of course, the Mother was never wrong. Today I am president," the president smiled as he thought to himself.

"Something happy, Sir?" Jason teased.

"Y-eah…y-es, Destroyer reminded me of an old cliché, that's all," the president readjusted himself.

Destroyer and the president discussed the past at length, and finally, the concerned statesman asked for what he had intended to ask from the start.

"I need you to tell me what we should be looking for. My people have come to their wit's end."

"Well, it is clear to me that the clues may be right in front of you," Moses offered.

"You mean…"

"Go back to the beginning. Whom did the investigation or the police talk to? What two or three statements looked like or had something in common, however remote? And above all, bad habits die hard; the Masterpiece is still nearer than you are looking…"

"Thank you, Destroyer, you have opened my eyes," the president abruptly ended the conversation and sent the Destroyer away with an envelope full of money.

When the Destroyer left the office, the president turned back to Jason and said, "Your turn, Sphinx, make the body disappear and the envelope reappear."

"As good as done, father."

"Hmm, what did you call me?"

"Oh, I said father. You know, you've been like a father to me."

"Oh, that's right, Jason, that's right."

***

It was all hands-on deck in the presidential universe. The president had created a clandestine group he called the "Night Watch," comprising old intelligence and retired secret servicemen, prosecutors, professors of law enforcement, retired judges, and an assortment of various experts in espionage investigations and counterintelligence operations. They worked when everyone else went to sleep.

After about four weeks of concerted efforts, they settled on a clue found in the police files of a person of interest called Melody Chanda. She could also be going by the name "Melody Mbewe," according to other records. When they investigated her, they found no records of the birth of such a person in Chambishi Township or any such person or relatives in Mushinge of Chief Mwendapole in Bemba land.

Suspicions also swelled when they gathered surveillance footage from Farm #7987511 in Lusaka West. They learned that Bishop Mwendashi's private vehicle had been seen entering and leaving the ranch, and the stables were relatively unengaged for a ranch of that size. When pizza was ordered from that address and location, a secret service agent posed as a pizza delivery man but was not allowed to reach the house; a botanist came to collect the pizza at the gate. These and other suspicions gave the Night Watch confidence that something was happening at that location.

Meanwhile, the Night Watch faced a challenge in designing the best way to attack the hacienda. They vacillated between air, ground, or underground operations. They finally agreed to use all simultaneously, making it the biggest operation Zambia had ever conducted.

As the day of the operation neared, Lucky Mwenda, the leader of the Night Watch, went to State House to brief the president. When he reached the house, he met the president in the People's Office. The meeting went well, and he left. Shortly after he left, another person who looked exactly like Lucky went to State House to meet the president. That evening the president met and addressed the Night Watch.

"Your operation has been compromised. Footage taken at State House revealed that the man I talked to was not Lucky. We, unfortunately, arrested Lucky but then released him when his identity was confirmed," the president addressed.

Then the president made an order that nobody would have expected under those conditions.

"We are not suspending the operation, tough men and women. We invade the ranch tomorrow night."

Meanwhile, Lucky Mwenda and his family were relocated to a safe house. But just as the president and his motorcade were leaving the Night Watch, Monde came up in his presidential Volvo holding a baby boy and said, "Hi, Father, I am well, and this is your first grandchild. By the way, you will kill us both if you trade Farm #7987511."

"Stop the motorcade!" the president ordered. "Let's go back!"

As the presidential motorcade turned in the opposite direction, the visibly rattled statesman was sweating profusely and attempting to loosen his necktie. He reached into his left jacket pocket and pulled out his cellphone.

"Jason, can you hear me?"

"Yes, Sir."

"Tell me you haven't fixed the Destroyer yet?"

"I…we did, Mr. President, at your instructions…"

"It's too late," the president spoke to himself rather than to Jason.

"What did you say, Sir?"

"Never mind, it's not important anymore."

The president just hung up his phone. He did not even say bye as he normally did when he finished talking to his political adviser, the man who literally ensured a landslide victory in his campaign.

The president remembered that he was going back to meet the Night Watch without prior notice.

"Call Lucky for me," he ordered his presidential motorcade driver.

"Yes, Sir."

When the driver called the stored number, it had been disconnected. The president also heard that the number was no longer in use.

"Oh, my bad, Lucky is in hiding," again, the president spoke more to himself than to those around him.

"Jason, find out who's taken over from Lucky Mwenda," the president made another call to his Chief of Staff.

After about ten minutes, Jason responded, "It's Jody Phiri, Sir," and he texted her contact number.

That day, Jason learned that the president would give an order to the Night

Watch to stop the manhunt and that he would disband the clandestine night junta.

Jason was not happy.

But that night the president could not meet with the Night Watch again either. They had been given a night off to unwind and be ready for "life or death" the following night. But Jody would "assemble the watchers at 10:00 tomorrow morning and we will meet up with you, Sir."

THE MAST – BREAKING NEWS

> This morning the nation woke up to real good news: The Boss is dead!
> A secret task force headed by the president himself has been working tirelessly and hard to get The Boss, dead or alive.
> In the wee hours of this morning, the reclusive The Boss was gunned down in cold blood.
> The nation can finally rest from relentless fear that man had inflicted upon the good citizens of Zambia...

President Zeibous was hailed as a hero. In the parliamentary elections that followed that year, the ruling PPD party returned with a majority in parliament, and Vice-president, Gabriella Munalula, was reinstalled as the leader of the House.

***

The death of The Boss saw another miracle happen at the Grand Cathedral. It was the rescue of Monde Mwendashi.

"My daughter will not be giving a testimony or media interviews. As you can see, the one-year-plus absence can be very devastating psychologically," Bishop Mwendashi announced to the congregation.

When rumors began to surge that Monde looked as if she had had a baby, many people dismissed it as the effects of being held in captivity for a long time.

"They definitely gave her poor food, and she must have gained some weight," one brother from Grand Cathedral commented.

The rumor did not last long. It quickly died down. Then, what Elder Mullen called a "Monde Revival" hit the Grand Cathedral. Not only did the Lusaka headquarters branch experience this, but branches began to open all across the nation. Television views of the "Grand Hour" grew. There were many additions to the numbers and the finances of the ministry. By the end of that year, the Monde Revival had become a phenomenon. Monde herself had become an icon, a star. Everywhere she went, people recognized her. When she preached, souls were saved in great numbers.

"God works in mysterious ways," a Zambia Daily Mail reporter started in an editorial. "When they kidnapped her and she spent over a year in captivity, no one could guess that she was the seed of greatness and growth they had planted in the ground to reap a hundredfold."

Benettes Mukonka quickly cleaned herself and changed her bloody attire.

"It's my ninety-ninth victim," she praised herself.

Benettes lived in Kalingalinga Compound near the University of Zambia (UNZA) when she was a little girl. She survived by selling vegetables and fruits to UNZA residents. She was called UNZA Veg.

After the UNZA administration banned all UNZA veggies, she had no option but to join the Lusaka street kid cohort. She was abused verbally, sexually, and mentally. One day, a man stopped with a Mercedes Benz car and asked her to wash it for him. After she washed it, she was given K500. That man came again and again. Benettes kept cleaning the car and getting rewarded.

Then one day, the same man asked if Benettes could join him for lunch. She did. During lunch at the Arcade Shopping Mall, Benettes was asked if she could join the Fraternity.

"What is the Fraternity?" Benettes had asked.

"It's an organization of similar-interested people," the man had replied.

"And what does this organization do?" she sought clarification.

"We kill people," the man had answered.

"Which people?" she asked.

"All people we are told to kill."

"I want to join to kill people," she had offered.

"Why?" the man had asked.

"Because those who kill people are better than those who don't."

"And why do you say so, Benettes?" the man asked.

"It's obvious, isn't it? You gave me a job, money, and food. I had never received these from those who don't kill people before."

"Mhm...hmm...excellent answer...I didn't expect it, got me unaware."

From then, Benettes was recruited. Within two months of her recruitment, she had already killed five people, which became a new record in the Fraternity. She was barely 13 years old. By the time she was 19 years old, she had killed over 3,000 people. The Fraternity nicknamed her "The Girl Killer" because she presented herself as a sociable girl but was, in fact, a very vicious assassin.

When she met Jason Mundiyah, he despised her.

"I paid them so much money, why would the Fraternity send me this nibling-looking sweet girl?"

To test her, he had assigned her to terminate Dr. Deborah Müller, a mixed Zambian-German doctor at the Sherbrooke Hospital in the Makeni area in Lusaka. Her late husband, a British politician, Vincent Sherbrooke, had established the hospital in Zambia when he visited the country some 35 years ago.

The target had provided the chemical compound that Jason had taken when he did DNA testing to prove that he was related to Monde Mwendashi's deceased father, whom he claimed was his brother.

"You must take half a teaspoon of this chemical within ten minutes before the test," she had instructed.

Prior, she had asked for Monde's DNA, which Jason had collected when Monde threw away a disposable coffee cup. Dr. Müller had sent Monde's and Jason's DNA samples to a specialized clinic in Germany, which concocted a chemical fluid Jason had drunk.

"You must kill Dr. Deborah Müller. Do a clean job. If you fail, it should be linked back to you, not to me. Here is the photo of the target."

It was the policy of the Fraternity to provide an assassin but not to issue instructions to them. Jason had accepted the terms.

Benettes had entered the clinic pretending to be a patient from a rich family. Her registration indicated that she was Beauty Mbulo, aged twenty-one years old. But when everyone was looking, she sneaked cyanide poison into Dr. Müller's coffee. Dr. Müller died at home in her bed.

Jason was very impressed. From then, he greatly trusted Benettes, whom he hired again to kill Monde.

"I know it's your profession not to know the reason for termination, you don't want to know why?" Jason had asked Benettes.

"No, sir. I am fine."

"But I'll tell you regardless."

"No need, sir."

"It's because she is my sister. She's the president's daughter just like I am his son."

"Oh, how come, sir? Now that you've told me."

"My mother was a prostitute. The last man she had slept with, according to her, was our president. Then, he worked for the intelligence wing. To prove that I was his son, my late mother had done DNA testing, which proved me to be his son. But when she challenged him, he had my mother and me shot. My mother died, but I survived. I was taken to an orphanage and was then adopted by a rich family, the Mundiyahs. "

"Does your father, I mean, the president, know that you're his son?"

"No, he doesn't. He thought that he had eliminated the evidence."

"So, the target…"

"I think I know what you want to ask. Yes, she shouldn't live to inherit his huge wealth. I should have it all."

"No, that's not what I wanted to ask, but it's fine. See you, sir. I must be going."

"Benettes…clean…do a clean job…"

"Patron, the order has been given. I have to do it by tomorrow night. I'll do as planned."

"We've got it ready. Dorothy will play a fake Monde. Monde is being prepared right now as I speak. You'll strike her right when she gets the audience excited; that way, her fake death will have credibility," ordered the Boss Boy.

"I have something else, Patron..."

"What's it, Benettes?"

"I learned that Jason is the illegitimate son of the president. His mother was killed by the president, but Jason survived. That's why he has a limp on his left leg."

"That's why he wants Monde out?"

"Yes, for inheritance..."

"Mhm...it makes more sense now..."

"And one more thing, Patron..."

"Huh?"

"The president doesn't know all that Jason has done to reach where he is...except..."

"Except for the president's own errands."

"So, do you have the recording?"

"Yes, Patron. Check your mobile, Sir."

The president's men, what a sham. They have not the slightest idea that my father owns the Fraternity. Ignorance is their greatest enemy, Mwanga, head of the Fraternity-in-principle, thought.

[14] THE PLAN

" I called you all here to make an announcement," The Boss began, "I am now more than any other time confident that I should take a layback approach to business."

The library was packed with all the notable people in the Arrogance Cartel. The only one notably absent among the original founders was Benjamin Kalasa, codenamed Shokashoka.

"And before I make the announcement, I wish to call on David Mpundu, our Chief Accountant, to give us the rundown of our accounts."

When David disclosed the profit margin of the business, it baffled everyone. The heroin business had tripled its profits since the hunt. The cocaine business had quadrupled. And methamphetamine was up to the roof, "owing to our recent partnership with our sister cartel, the Masvingo Cartel in Namibia."

Khat had been recently introduced to the cartel, so no report was given. "But marijuana consumption has greatly reduced owing to the decriminalization of the drug. We are still trying to plot the correlation between legalizing marijuana and its consumption."

Then David revealed the number that everyone was interested in.

"We made over US$303.5 billion in all drug categories in this fiscal year. We continued to do well in real estate, with US$120 billion profit. Our supermarkets and malls together earned us US$219 billion. We gave back to the community in incognito and unanimous donations about US$290 billion. And should I say, it was all due to the effective and wise leadership of

Boss Mwanga, even when The Boss was imprisoned."

The room full of people gave a standing ovation to Boss Boy, and all of them saluted him for the extraordinary work he had done. That gave The Boss the opportunity he was looking for to disclose what he had earlier indicated.

"And that is why I have resigned as head of the cartel; my son is now the new Boss and head of the Arrogance Cartel. Everyone, give him the same support you have been giving me."

The people nodded at The Boss' resignation, but with misgivings. Some had never known any other person as their leader since they were young. Others were recruited from backgrounds they could not look back on. And still, others had suffered through thick and thin with The Boss.

"Boss, I hope you will still be available for us, to counsel us and give us guidance when we feel lost, as you have always done," pleaded Melody, and as she did, almost everyone said, "Yes, yes, please."

As they shared a cocktail of drinks and snacks, The Boss gave a sign that he wanted to say something very personal.

They all stopped what they were doing and listened.

"To the new Boss, the team, and every family here, this is my last plea. Please do everything to free my best friend and co-prisoner, Benjamin the Shokashoka. That would be my send-off to my grave with a smile on my face."

The whole group in unison held hands and shouted, "We will, even if it is the last thing we do before our very own lives."

And after they had all eaten and danced, the time came for the new Boss to give his speech.

Dressed in the blue jeans Monde had just bought for him, and holding his three-year-old son, Mwanga stepped into the center of the circle and said,

"As you all know, I am now a Christian. As I read the Holy Bible recently, I came across a verse that I believe is germane to my comment today: 'I believed; therefore, I have spoken,' (2 Corinthians 4:13). Let everyone gathered here know that I believe in what I am going to say. And what I say is this: I am going to make Zambia the drug capital of Africa."

After saying that, Mwanga sat down.

Everyone stood up and gave him a standing ovation. Some commented, "He's always been a man of very few words," others echoed, "Like his father, The Boss, action speaks louder than words!"

"I thought that this would be the most mature way of trying to resolve conflicts," Bishop Mwendashi clarified her position and the reason why she had called the meeting between The Boss and President Zeibous.

But already there were tensions. Just agreeing on the venue was a hassle. Mumbwa South was picked as a venue because of its significance to the two former best friends. It was at the Mumbwa Lodge some 50-plus years ago where they sequestered themselves with wines and champagnes for their activities in espionage. They had become the first Zambian secret service members to literally bring the British reign to a halt.

Both the government and the Arrogance Cartel had sent spies to secure the area for potential hazards. They were not taking anything for granted.

In the kitchen, the Zeibous people and the cartel's members had inspected every utensil, cutlery, drink, furniture, seat, room, etc., to ensure that the place was safe.

Both leaders pretended to sip their drinks, but they didn't actually drink.

"Fearing poison?" The Boss teased.

"It is routine in my line of work," the president said.

It looked like the day before when the two shared just about everything. They shared food, drink, clothing, weapons, games, shelter, yes, even a woman. There they were being suspicious of everything and everyone around them.

"Okay, gentlemen, I will reiterate the ground rules I sent to each one of you prior. First, there will be no disturbing each other when given the chance to speak…"

It was The Boss who interrupted the mediator and said, "I have them here, I am sure the president has…"

"Yes, I also have them. Skip the obvious."

Bishop Mwendashi felt like she was mediating between power and money.

"Oh, God have mercy. Don't you guys miss the time when we had neither; nor life was so much easier although we thought otherwise?"

There were at least some nods from both sides, albeit short-lived. Then began the finger-pointing. And it was the president who started.

"Your cartel is the cancer of this nation. You are polluting the minds and bodies of the youth with prohibited substances..."

"Hold it there, Holier than Thou, and you are cheating people each day while, through corruption and vanity, you leave them wallowing in poverty..."

"Gentlemen," the bishop interrupted, "you are forgetting the purpose of this meeting. Be civil and talk about how we can resolve this issue. Remember that you have one thing in common, your grandchild."

When the two heard the mention of their grandchild, they almost immediately calmed down. It was clear that they cared about the child very much.

"But you have denied me the chance to see my—"

"Hold on, Mr. President. I'm sure you can see on the agenda that he's here, and you will see him."

"Oh, Zeib, always impatient. No wonder nothing is working under your administration…"

"Stop, stop it, Mila…"

"You are still calling him by that name? Are you still in love with this—"

"Yes, she still loves me, even though you tried to steal her from me…"

"Guys, stop it. You're behaving like children!" The bishop was growing frustrated.

The three did not cooperate for the most part, but when a maid presented the almost five-year-old boy, they both jumped up and down like little boys. They both wanted the boy.

"To be fair, Mila, let Muka have him now. At least you have been seeing the baby boy…"

"Are you still after this guy, calling him Muka…"

"Stop it, Mila, stop it."

That last rebuke from the bishop calmed the situation down. The new grandparents found common ground in the baby boy. They teased, tickled, and hugged him. They were beside themselves, especially the president, who was seeing the baby for the first time.

For a while, the rivalry between them seemed to subside. But when Monde was introduced, the atmosphere changed.

"I can't believe you have neglected your own child like that..." Monde lashed out at the president, who remained silent. It was the bishop who defended him.

"No, it wasn't always like that. Before he became president, he actually saw you, but politics stopped all that, although he always provided..."

"Provided what, Mother? I found out that he was my father through grapevine talk on television. How embarrassing. And providing food is not the same as love..."

"But I was also denied the chance to see and know my son..." they began to sob.

The daughter and her two past lovers hugged and embraced her. It was so emotional that the four literally forgot about the formalities and protocols. The president and The Boss poured each other some champagne and drowned their bitter rivalry. The mother and daughter stuck to lemonade.

"This doesn't mean that what you are doing in your cartel will be forgiven," the president said, throwing it at The Boss.

"And you, with all the murders..." The Boss was interrupted.

"Which murders?" The president began to get defensive.

The bishop knew that if she lost it there, the meeting would be disastrous.

"Gentlemen, we all know there is much animosity between you two. This is only the first meeting, so let's keep it strictly family.

God willing, we shall have other meetings to address issues and politics."

She was quiet for most of the meeting, but it didn't take a genius to observe the tension between the president and Monde. The president was all smiles, even blushing, but Monde appeared troubled. When she saw an opening in the conversation, she spoke up.

"I don't know if I should address you as Mr. President or Zeibous; it seems you prefer ambition to relationships..."

"Monde..." The bishop tried to intervene.

"No, Mother, leave this between me and him. He's an adult and can answer for himself."

"Mm..." Bishop Mwendashi paused.

"So, what is it?" Monde directed her question to the president.

"I... I... t-this... no..." President Zeibous was at a loss for words.

"You speak so fluently on national and international television. I'm sure you can answer me just fine," Monde mocked.

"You know what, you're right. I'm sorry…" began the president.

"Sorry for what?" Monde pressed.

"Sorry because politics have taken over my life, and I've neglected my own daughter," the president said directly. His honesty somewhat unsettled Monde, who had expected him to beat around the bush.

"He is so direct and genuine. Does this mean he truly cares about me? Of course, he's done everything for my decency and well-being. I think I should give him credit…" Monde thought.

"Did I say something offensive, ma'am?" The president asked.

"No, no, sir. But why didn't you want to see or meet me?" Monde asked politely.

"Indeed, I haven't met you officially since your fifth birthday, but I see you every day. My secret agents send me images of you from time to time…"

"Are you stalking me?"

"On the contrary. I love you so much that if anything were to happen to you, I would lose myself. Look…"

The president opened his phone and began to share photos and videos of Monde from when she was ten years old, essentially covering his entire presidency. Monde and her mother were surprised, but The Boss was disappointed, especially when Bishop Mwendashi looked at him from the corner of her eye, as if saying, "See, you should have done the same for Mwanga."

Then The Boss reached into his left jacket pocket and retrieved an envelope.

"Look," the president said, "this is my will. See who is the sole beneficiary of all that I have and own…" He handed the envelope to the bishop, who perused it and smiled before handing it over to Monde.

Monde reluctantly accepted it and began to read.

"All this is mine?" Monde asked, excitedly.

"Yes, ma'am," the president confirmed.

"And why are you calling me 'ma'am'?" Monde inquired.

"What should I call you, ma'am?"

"Daughter, Princess, or Queen, like my mother does!"

"I wanted to earn it. I know I owe you more… Isn't it so, Princess, since I am president?" The president joked.

Monde blushed irresistibly, moved over to her father, and hugged him tightly while sobbing silently.

"All I wanted was a relationship with my own father, not money and all these things," Monde said.

"I know, and I am sorry, Princess. Do you want to know why I didn't want to put you in the spotlight?"

"Yes, but I think I know—because of politics, right?"

"Yes. We have many enemies…" President Zeibous glanced at The Boss mockingly.

"Uh-huh, Monde, go. Leave us alone for a while," The Boss instructed.

After Monde left, the bishop held the hands of the two men and said, "Can't you see that you two have more in common?"

"I know, but I can't just stand by while Bwembya destroys our country with drugs. Not on my watch," President Zeibous stated.

"Brother, you go out there desecrating my name as if I have wronged you. In fact, I am highly forgiving and loving. For you, Beatrice, I castrated myself. And for you, Zeib, do you want proof that I am the only person in this country who keeps your presidential dreams? Look…"

What The Boss showed them next took the wind out of the president. It was a rollercoaster of corruption, murder, conspiracies, contempt, and bribery that made the bishop run to the washroom to vomit.

"I…I…I mean, you've had all this all this time?"

"Yes, Brother. If I wanted to destroy you, it would have been as simple as pressing a button."

"But why didn't you expose him…" began the bishop, who had just returned from the washroom.

"…despite putting me in jail, tarnishing my character and integrity in public, ordering a manhunt for me, and even a death sentence… it's because I believe in principle and the right timing. You know that after I was unceremoniously rejected by the Mother, your mother, Beatrice, I realized that Zeibous was also a victim, in fact, a prisoner of his own conscience."

"How so?" Bishop Mwendashi probed.

"You haven't asked him… Zeib., should you tell her someday?" The Boss insisted.

"I feel so ashamed, Brother, that even when I did all kinds of evil against you, you still honored the oath…"

"What oath? I'm lost here…" Bishop Mwendashi inquired.

The president began to sob. The Boss reached into his pocket and offered him a handkerchief.

"I will have it, Brother. You mean well to me. You're the only person who can't poison me…"

"You Boys are not making sense to me. Just last week, you were like sworn enemies, and now you're behaving like two boys who've sworn fealty to one another…"

"Yes, because we did, you can't see. I broke mine, but he kept his. You can't see that, Beatrice; he's a good man I have been greedily trying to destroy—except, of course, for the drug trade," President Zeibous lashed out at Bishop Mwendashi.

Both The Boss and the bishop were speechless at that moment. After wiping his tears, the president asked The Boss, "What must I do, Brother?"

"Here's what I came up with. Take it or leave it. You must resign and hand over the presidency to a decent person, then accept a prison sentence as I have done. I accepted prison as atonement—you know that. Otherwise, no one can imprison me. I just thought it was excessive, which is why I escaped. But you…"

"I have not been punished for my atrocities… you are not incorrect, Brother. But whom do I give the presidency to? Maybe Jason; he's been very loyal to me…"

"Hold your speech, Brother. Jason is your number one enemy. He's surrendered his soul to the devil. He's even manipulated his own DNA to try and disinherit Monde…"

"What are you talking about, Brother?" President Zeibous asked, desperately.

"Just look…" The Boss showed the president a video of Jason's shenanigans. The president collapsed and fainted.

"Welcome to State House, Mr. Kaitano Chanda. The president is waiting for you in the People's Office."

"Thank you, Mr. Jason Mundiyah. Please lead the way."

"Follow me, kindly."

The president was pacing the floor, clearly troubled. He needed to get something off his chest.

"I must relinquish my position and take responsibility," he said, speaking to himself.

Just then, there was a knock on the door.

"Come in," the president invited.

Both Kaitano and Jason entered.

"I must ask you to leave us momentarily, Jason. I want to talk to Mr. Chanda alone."

The order struck Jason hard; he almost fell. It was the first time his boss had asked him to miss a conversation. He was rattled.

"S-sure, Mr. President," Jason choked.

As he walked to the door, he looked back and winced, but the president remained standing where Jason had left him. This disoriented him.

"Has the president found out what I have been up to? Did my plan get exposed? Am I in trouble? What if he tells Chanda? I'm screwed..." Jason thought about every possibility in milliseconds.

He let himself out but then remained outside the double doors, peeking through the crevices to hear what was being discussed in the People's Office. When the first secretary, Jane Lunde, arrived with tea for the NGC leader, she found Jason peeking and thought it was odd.

"Excuse me, Mr. Political Advisor," Jane said as she passed him to deliver the tea tray. Jason pretended to drop his cellphone and looked for it. Realizing it wouldn't fool the first secretary, he composed himself and left.

After Jane left, the president resumed his conversation with Kaitano Chanda.

"As I was about to say, I am considering you to take over as president..."

Kaitano was caught off guard, jerking slightly before recomposing himself.

"Mr. President..."

"Please, hear me out. I am neither delusional nor unhinged. I am absolutely sane. But I have considered the nation's best interest..."

"What's the catch, Mr. President?"

"I need you to promise me a fair plea deal. I have committed many crimes and feel unfit to continue as president. If you accept my deal, I would like you to retain Madam Vice-President Gabriella in the government of national unity and…"

"And what, Mr. President?"

"And my daughter, Monde Mwendashi, as your political advisor."

"Sir, Monde is your daughter?"

"Hmm…"

"You mean the vibrant young daughter of Bishop Mwendashi?"

"Yep, my very own flesh and blood."

"Sir, it will be my exceptional honor," Kaitano said, going down on his left knee while holding the president's right hand. He was beside himself with joy.

"It's fine, stand up now," the president said.

Kaitano Chanda stood up, trembling, and then inquired, "When do you anticipate this transition, Mr. President, and why did you choose me and not the DNA party?"

"Hm-hmm, good question. Well, you are untainted by corruption, you represent the young generation who believe in ethical politics, and I have observed you. You have leadership qualities and love this nation. Is that enough?"

"Yes, it is for me. I promise to give you a fair deal. If this goes through, you will be remembered as a true hero…"

"Don't go there, Kaitano. Until I tell you what I have done, you'll think even the devil himself is a saint. I will reveal my sins when the time is right."

"I understand, Sir."

"Won't you ask me to put this in writing so that I keep my word?"

"Oh, that… you're right, Mr. President."

***

Dubbed "The Wedding of the Century," Monde shined like a star in a white wedding dress, holding red and white roses. Her groom, the new boss of the Arrogance Cartel, was decked out like a knight in a golden tuxedo.

The marriage was officiated at the Grand Cathedral by Rev. Mullen, who had recently been ordained as clergy after leading the Elders Council for more than twenty years. Bishop Mwendashi had recused himself due to a secret known only to a few.

"We will not tell anyone in the church until later, perhaps, to protect my children and the integrity of the church," the bishop had told me, the president, and The Boss.

However, this secret was vulnerable to the machinations of Jason, who was determined to ruin the reputation of the Grand Cathedral, the bishop, and, more importantly, Monde. Jason's plan to target Monde had failed; the Fraternity reported that the Girl Assassin had been killed by one of Monde's bodyguards, who also died in the exchange. Jason was refunded the entire retainer he had paid to the Fraternity. When he asked for a new assassin, the Fraternity excused itself, citing timing.

"We will not be prepared to assign one at this moment. The target is a high-profile figure, and people may be suspicious at this time," the Fraternity's secretary responded in part. This was a major reason why the bishop had said "to protect my children."

The ceremony was held at the renowned Intercontinental Hotel loft, with only a select few guests in attendance. There was massive security detail due to the threat from Jason's men. On the wedding day, the president had assigned Jason to attend the Mutomboko Ceremony on his behalf, which coincided with the wedding.

"Old man, what can I get for you?" a waitress asked.

"I think a raspberry twist will do for now," responded a grey-haired man who appeared to be in his late seventies.

As the man received his glass of raspberry juice, he silently raised a glass in cheers to the bride and groom, who did the same. The old man then quietly disappeared.

The groom turned to his wife and whispered, "He looks good in those disguises; what do you think?"

"Yeah, at first I couldn't even remotely recognize him," she said.

"Alright, now about our PLAN?" Mwanga reminded.

"It remains as we discussed. You must clean the business as soon as possible. It will take time because of its size, but begin..."

"But...but..."

"But what, Mwanga?"

"When I told Dad..."

"You told him about this?"

"I mean, it was a hypothetical question..."

"So?"

"I wanted to hear his opinion first, you know, whether we like it or not, he created it and risked his life for it."

"I know, Mwanga, but we must do God's will, remember?"

"I understand. But where do I take all that money? Remember, we didn't conclude on that one?"

"I had a revelation on that. Give back four times to the nation; let's call it the 'Zaccheus Mission'—remember the short tax collector who climbed up the tree to see Jesus..."

"I do. He gave back all that he owed to the poor fourfold... but I do have a concern..."

"What is it, Mwanga?"

"The Zambia Revenue Agency (ZRA) and my employees…"

"You're right. ZRA will want to investigate the source of the money, and employees shouldn't be left indigent. I know what we should do for both of those concerns."

"Really?"

"I do. Just trust me on that one."

"Okay, Monde, let's now go and dance on the floor, shall we?"

"Let's go!"

[15] DEATH OF THE BISHOP

"I need to talk to the Patron; it's urgent," Benettes insisted as Melody tried various lines to get through to Mwanga.

"His line is either off or someone is holding it and not picking up," Melody tried to calm Benettes.

"But can you get through to The Boss or the Bishop, please? Their lives could be in danger," Benettes was unfazed.

Benettes had overheard Jason instructing an assassin from other sources to eliminate Monde's mother at the same time as he was sending Benettes to kill Monde at the hotel.

"Put the bomb in her plane," Jason had instructed the assassin.

Having tried unsuccessfully, Benettes called 911.

"How can I help you?" the dispatcher asked.

"The bishop is in danger. Please send a dispatch to prevent her from boarding her plane," Benettes said.

"But who are you, and how do you know that?" the dispatcher inquired.

"Can you just do what I'm telling you? Bishop Mwendashi is in danger, please."

"Ma'am, my mother is also in danger," the dispatcher did not take Benettes seriously.

"You... unprofessional and useless. Now you'll be responsible if something bad happens..." Benettes hung up the phone in disgust. At her wit's end, she googled the Grand Cathedral's website and found the number. When she called, it went to the answering machine: "We are closed. Our hours of operation are ten to five Monday to Friday, and seven to seven Saturday and Sunday. Please leave a message after the beep."

Benettes tried Mwanga's number again, and someone picked up.

"Hello, who's this?" Chisanshi asked.

"It's me, Benettes. It's urgent. Can I talk to the Patron, please?"

"I don't know you," Chisanshi said and hung up.

Benettes was undeterred. She called again. In fury and anger, Chisanshi answered and began to curse when he heard, "They are going to kill his mother-in-law…"

That got Chisanshi's attention.

"But who?" Chisanshi inquired.

"Does that matter? Just give the Patron the phone," Benettes said.

"He's gone. He's with his wife, if you know what I mean."

"I don't care. Push the door, do whatever you need to do. We're running out of time…"

"Okay, I will try my best…"

As Chisanshi was talking to Benettes on the phone, Monde and Mwanga appeared from their hotel room in nightgowns. The couple was visibly troubled.

"Chisanshi, check if what they're reporting on TV is true," Mwanga asked, holding his wife tightly because she was distraught.

Before Chisanshi could answer, Gertrude came crying and held her phone to Monde's ear. "They want to talk to you," she said, sobbing sporadically.

"We regret to inform you that…" the person on the phone began.

"What? Can you say it, please?" Monde ran out of patience.

"…the president and your mother have been killed in a plane crash."

Monde fainted. Mwanga heard but wasn't sure of what was said.

"Chisanshi, call Matafwali," Mwanga instructed.

"Yes, Sir."

Meanwhile, as they returned to their hotel room, the television was broadcasting breaking news.

"UNCONFIRMED REPORT INDICATES THAT PRESIDENT ZEIBOUS AND BISHOP MWENDASHI HAVE DIED IN A PLANE CRASH."

Before Mwanga could process what was happening, Chisanshi came and whispered in his ear, "There is bad news. Your father was also on that plane. Matafwali confirms that he's deceased…"

Mwanga collapsed onto the sofa. He realized it would be a scandal if both his parents died in the same plane crash.

"Chisanshi, ask the team to retrieve Father's body."

"They already did. Benettes got to them, and they were just minutes away from stopping the plane, but Polopela did not know…"

"Where is Dad's body now?"

"At the ranch; they are waiting for you there, Sir."

"CONSTITUTIONAL CRISIS IN ZAMBIA," headlined the *York News* in Ontario, Canada. Veep Gabriella Munalula had taken over as acting president pending the election of a new president in 90 days "pursuant to article 49 of the new constitution," the Canadian newspaper reported.

Chaos erupted when the leader of the NGC party presented a letter purportedly written by the late president to the Speaker of Parliament. Debate on the letter's legitimacy continued during the seven days of national mourning for the late bishop of the Grand Cathedral and President Zeibous. Once the letter was proven valid, a constitutional crisis ensued.

Factions in the country that supported the old constitution argued that Veep Munalula was the legitimate successor of the late president and should be honored. The other faction, led by Kaitano and Monde, insisted that the will of the late president was the only way forward and was in accordance with the new constitution.

Then, out of nowhere, a new party emerged, changing everything. The Global South Empowerment Party (GSRP) had been registered earlier but had not been formally introduced. Its leader, Jason Mundiyah, claimed both natural legitimacy and legal status to assume the presidency. To support his claim, he presented three documents to the Speaker of Parliament.

"The first document, Mr. Speaker, is the will executed by my father before his untimely death; the second is the letter he wrote and was witnessed by Ms. Jane Lunde, now deceased; and the last is an email Ms. Lunde sent to me and the secretary to the cabinet in witness to the president's wishes. How prescient my father must have been, anticipating this impasse after his untimely death."

Jason's speech silenced the debate. As he introduced himself as the late president's son, a massive national tsunami surged in Zambia.

"No one had any idea that the president had a son. In fact, apart from a fleeting rumor that Monde might be his biological son, people believed the late president had no children," commented Prof. Shaun Maga of the Zambian Open University, head of the political science department.

"And even if Mr. Mundiyah's claims were valid, Zambia is neither a traditional nor a constitutional monarchy; Zambia is a democracy," Prof. Moffat Nchoba of Lusaka University School of Law challenged.

The debate in Parliament and in the courts of public opinion saturated the nation for days until the acting Attorney General's Office launched a reference case with the Supreme Court of Zambia. The situation calmed slightly.

During the ten days of deliberations, the nation was almost ungovernable. Riots erupted in the major cities of Livingstone, Kitwe, and Mbala. Factions and their followers clashed openly. It became clear to the ten puisne justices and the Chief Justice that the evidence presented by the GSRP's leader was winning the case until a video miraculously surfaced online and went viral.

The prison had the same structure as the State House Prison, uprooted from its foundation. It had lost most of its luxury, but its functionality remained unchanged. A technician from the original construction company had been reemployed for maintenance.

That morning marked the first time a prisoner would occupy it. Seven hours had passed since he was thrown in. He had been stripped of all his clothes and left on the cold floor, with only a small bottle of warm water provided in his cell.

The cell had only one glass door, and it was transparent. This was the most noticeable difference between the original one, housed in State House, and the one located at the old Kalene Hacienda. Directly through the transparent door, Prisoner #3 could see a glass casket with an embalmed body. Dr. Phiri Sr. had attended to the casket at least four times over a span of four hours. He was referred to as Dr. Phiri because that was what everyone, including the cleaners, called him.

Later that week, Prisoner #0003 began to feel the psychological torture. Inside his cell, there was a plaque with Daniel 4:33 written on it: "Nebuchadnezzar was forced to go away from people, and he began eating grass like an ox. He became wet from dew. His hair grew long like the feathers of an eagle, and his nails grew like the claws of a bird."

After five days of consuming only water, a bag of grass was introduced into his cell. At first, he ignored it, but after two more days, he began to eat the grass and that became his sole diet. He was allowed to bathe using high-pressure water within the cell to eliminate bugs, germs, and bacteria, which made the cell wet. He was not permitted to shave his hair or cut his nails.

"He will look like a beast in four months," Dr. Vozansa Phiri, a pathologist, reported to his father, Dr. Phiri Sr.

"I see. And what about his diet?" Dr. Phiri Sr. inquired.

"He will adapt to survive, I think," the pathologist replied.

"What about his human consciousness? Will he retain it?"

"Yes, Father. He will always remember that he did something wrong for which he's being punished."

"That suffices for us."

The brilliance of the July weather brought with it a soothing southeasterly wind that made the air feel like air conditioning. Monde was still dressed in black as she walked toward her mother's tomb, which was adjacent to the late former president Zeibous' tomb.

She touched the edge of a golden cross that adorned her mother's tomb, with the statue of Jesus Christ's open tomb caricature she had designed for her mother's burial. Beneath the caricature was an epitaph that read: "I ran the race of faith, now a crown of righteousness awaits me and those who believe."

Curiously, she compared her mother's tomb to the one next to it. Its shape and architecture were elaborate. On it was a golden eagle in flight, with a coat of arms that greeted her inquisitive gaze. The epitaph there read: "Here lies the remains of gallantry and resolve. Rest in peace, 17th President of the Democratic Republic of Zambia, Zeibous Mwansa Zulu."

She touched it and wiped the dust that had gathered around the crown of the eagle. Laying her left hand on her mother's grave and her right hand on her father's, she shed tears and began to speak to them:

"You both died unexpectedly. I would have liked to have a longer, more meaningful relationship with you, Dad, as I did with you, Mother. But the earth decided that you should rest in heavenly peace here. Just know that my tears will never dry for you both. Mother, I am now your new successor, but I refused to take the title of bishop, for Zambia will always have only one Bishop, and it's you..."

Just then, a Secret Service agent clad in a black suit and black glasses approached Monde and whispered, "Madam Vice-President, President Chanda wants you at State House within an hour. It's urgent."

"Thanks, Mr. Guzu..."

"And... is there anything I can do for you, ma'am? Perhaps give a helping hand..."

"No, no, Mr. Guzu, I think I can manage on my own... but thank you for asking."

The Vice-President and her entourage left the Heroes Memorial Gardens Cemetery and headed for State House.

***

"Madam Vice-President?"

"I'm here, Your Excellency."

"I am sorry to disturb your sacred space with this urgent call. We still haven't found the impostor, Jason Mundiyah. Now I hear that there's a lead…"

"Mr. President, what's the nature of the lead, sir?"

"Honestly, ma'am, I don't know. To be frank, I didn't have the courage to handle it myself, so I called you to accompany me."

"Really, sir, I am honored."

The Vice-President was blatantly lying. In reality, she was taken aback. She knew that the nation's most wanted fugitive was in her husband's custody, but that was a secret the Arrogance Cartel was willing to go to war with the government to protect.

Oh, God, let this whistleblower not reveal the truth. I am still working on transforming the cartel into an economic asset to help the poor in Zambia. I pray, Lord, that you confuse the whistleblower in some way... she thought.

"Madam Vice-President, the whistleblower is in the situation room, formerly the operation room, waiting for you," the President's aide announced.

"Mr. President, you are our boss, our leader. After you, sir."

"If you say so, ma'am."

The duo arrived, and to Monde's relief, the whistleblower was none other than Benettes. She was calm and collected, and looked very believable. She and the Vice-President had met before at the Fraternity's office, where Mwanga had introduced her as "the best holy soldier of our lifetime."

"This is Mary Munthali, Madam Vice-President. She knows where the fugitive could be hidden."

"Thanks, Your Excellency. May I…"

"Yes, yes, yes. Please, the floor is yours, ma'am," the President said, without hesitation.

With a glance, the whistleblower and the Vice-President, her most admired woman, were face to face. They immediately shared a symbolic gesture by raising their left index fingers. Monde knew that Mary Munthali, also known as Benettes, was not being credible. She was trying to protect the Vice-President.

And how did he do it? Mwanga can read my mind. In one blow, he's trying to distance me from suspicion, and in the other, keep Jason in the national spotlight. But why? she thought.

"Madam Vice-President, Mr. President, you asked me to gather clues about the fugitive because I worked closely with him and know how he maneuvered. I think I have something to share."

"Please tell us," the Vice-President urged her on.

"Thank you, Ma'am. I received a tip from an old neighbor of his who had previously done maintenance on his Siavonga cottage near the Karina Dam. So, I followed the lead."

"And what did you find?"

"Yes, Ma'am. I discovered that he had been there recently. There were leftover no-name pizzas which could be no more than three weeks old. This corresponds to the period when the army concentrated their search in Luapula Province..."

"I remember seeing those reports then," President Chanda admitted.

"So, what do we do now?"

"Yes, Ma'am. I will keep an eye on this location without drawing too much attention."

"That's good. Meanwhile, I will also maintain a team around his Muchinga

Mountain lodge. Thanks, Mary. You have opened my eyes. We were looking in all the wrong places."

[16] THE CORRONATION

Dorothy remembered that fateful evening when they arrived at the scene of the wreckage a bit late to save The Boss. He was barely breathing. Then he had whispered to her as she held his head with a mangled body.

"Y-o-u m-u-s-t t-e-l-l m-y s-o-n t-o b-u-r-y m-e o-n-l-y a-f-t-e-r r-e-s-c-u-I-n-g B-Benji," then he passed away right in her arms.

She, and the Team, had no time to waste and because the president had perished in a private plane, it would be a scandal to report that the then number one enemy of the state also died from the same plane crash. That fact still remained classified. However, since the bishop was the official adviser to the presidency on religious affairs, it would not be a scandal.

In fact, during the state funeral, Rev. Paul Mvula of the Redeemed Church of Zambia (RCZ) gave the following eulogy in his prayer:

"Father, in your infinite wisdom, you gave us yet another sign that the leadership of this Christian nation is yours. For the president of this nation has been guided by your holy servant even into the very presence of God..."

That line prompted everyone to stand and give a sustained round of applause during the funeral mass at the Grand Cathedral's Eunice Mukupo Chapel. The chapel was named after Eunice Mukupo, who had died during the construction process when debris had fallen upon her. Her family had considered it a blessing and chose not to sue, despite advice from many lawyers.

During Eunice's funeral, held in an empty field because the building was still under construction, her father, Dave Mukupo, said, "We send our sixteen-year-old daughter to the gate of heaven with the hope that in her death, we might achieve the salvation of many souls in this place."

The father's prayer had moved the board of directors, who unanimously decided to name the chapel after Eunice.

The president and the bishop had died instantly in the explosion. The Boss, however, was still breathing when the team arrived. He died an hour later after being removed from the wreckage. His son and successor, Mwanga, ordered that his remains be embalmed until his best friend, Benjamin "Shokashoka," was freed from prison.

When tasked with the mission to free Shokashoka, the team weighed all options. The government was no longer the cartel's enemy; in fact, it was seen more as a partner. Mwanga's only instructions to the team, under Dorothy's direct order, were: "Do not embarrass the government. Make it flawless. And I don't want my wife to know what is going on. She's part of the government now." The mission was codenamed the "Dorothea Dream."

"Morgan, you will bribe an inmate to sneak a pill into Shokashoka's drink," Dorothy instructed.

"On it, thanks," Morgan Mulopwe replied, ready.

"Nalu, you will impersonate Dr. Henry Kantumoyo, head of the infirmary, and certify Shokashoka's death."

"I am on it," Nalumino Pemba assured.

"Katuta, make sure to drill the grave site to remove the subject alive."

"On it as well."

The budget for the operation was the largest the cartel had ever seen, amounting to US$1.1 million. The operation was conducted over a period of three months after all preparations were complete.

The day of the operation was not communicated to Shokashoka himself. He woke up as usual and went for his cell-made coffee. He told his cellmate, Anvil Chola, that he was not feeling well. Within an hour, his condition worsened. Anvil called the officer on duty, who recommended that Shokashoka be taken to the infirmary for closer observation. After arriving at the infirmary, Dr. Kantumoyo pronounced him dead.

The cause of death was listed as "food poisoning" attributed to coffee. The coroner was not required to perform an autopsy, and the deceased was cleared for immediate burial. Wrapped in a white cloth, the body was taken to the cemetery for inmates in the Chilanga area and buried there with the assigned plot number 7098.

That same night, the team exhumed the body and replaced it with a stone.

"Where am I?" Shokashoka asked, surprised and a bit dazed.

"Shh, you're in good hands. You need to relax now," Dr. Phiri Jr. advised.

Shokashoka was under medical observation for the entire day. The next morning, the first person he saw was Mwanga.

"Boss, Boss, what happened to me? I just found myself in this nice…"

"…room, yes. It's now yours. Your best friend, Dad, could not have left it for a more deserving person…"

"Where's The Boss? Why would he give me such a good room?"

"He's waiting for you when you are ready."

"I am ready. I have missed him dearly. Can we go now?"

"Yes, we may go."

As they approached the elevator leading to the underground tunnel, Shokashoka saw a recent newspaper with his name on it.

"Look, sir, it says here that I died?" he asked Mwanga, but expected anyone in the retinue to respond.

"You are now resurrected, probably the first Zambian to do so!" Mwanga said jokingly, and everyone in the retinue laughed.

"So, you…"

"Yes."

"At the instruction of The…"

"…Boss, yes."

Shokashoka was in high spirits as the conversation with his boss's son made him feel like a hero. When they arrived at Kalene Hacienda, he was taken into a cold room, and the first person he met there was an old but familiar face.

"Martin! I remember you; you are that doctor…" Shokashoka exclaimed.

"Yes, Benjamin…"

Before Dr. Phiri Sr. could swallow his saliva, the two were in each other's arms, hugging. Tears began to pour down Dr. Phiri Sr.'s cheeks.

"What's wrong, Henry?"

Dr. Phiri Sr. did not say another word. He pointed with his chin to the casket behind the recently freed henchman.

Shokashoka knew something was amiss. He rushed over to the casket where they had laid his Boss and best friend. He dropped to his knees and sobbed uncontrollably. They allowed him to mourn his friend without interruption.

***

It was described as the coronation of the century. In attendance were over ninety percent of the Zambian clergy, the ruling NGC party, opposition parties, and various public and private stakeholders.

When she appeared and took her seat on the podium, Monde chose a peripheral seat, which was the first surprise. The second surprise was that, instead of being decked investments, she wore only black trousers and a jacket suit.

The moment everyone was waiting for arrived, and Elder Mullen introduced her with, "It's now my honor to welcome Madam Vice-President to give her remarks."

Many people, especially those who had not witnessed her mother, the late Bishop Mwendashi's ordination, did not notice any difference. However, the older attendees immediately sensed something was amiss.

"Monde is so reserved; she's not after titles and pomp," one attendee commented.

"Don't be too quick to judge. She's a politician now; she knows how to manipulate people to ingratiate herself with corruption. Just wait," another countered.

When Monde took the mic, every notable media house in Zambia was attentively present.

"I gladly accept the role as the leader of the Grand Cathedral, but I relinquish the title of bishop. I believe I am not capable of filling my late mother's shoes. Instead, I will accept the title of Senior Elder Emeritus in honor of the work and to preserve the vision that my mother worked tirelessly to create by the grace of God…"

Everyone stood and gave a standing ovation. Sitting in the television booth with his young son, Mwanga clapped with his right hand while his left held onto the boy.

"That's your mother, isn't she great?" Mwanga said.

"Mmm…she is…but, Dad, why didn't she take us there with her?" his son asked.

"It's complicated, Son."

"But, Dad, what's more important than family?"

"You're right. It's because of family that she decided to make us wait a bit…"

"That means we will join her there, too?"

"Perhaps, lad…perhaps. Let's listen; your mother is continuing to speak."

Monde took a sip from the bottle of water placed for her convenience and continued.

"What I am about to reveal may not shock the nation, but it will make me resign from the very position I am being ordained for today…" she began.

A hush fell over the audience. There was no movement, and even the cameramen stood at attention. People took out their phones, preparing to record not only her voice but also the video.

"My mother was not a saint; God rest her soul. Neither am I. Everyone remembers a rumor that emerged seven years ago about me being the daughter of the late President Zeibous. It's true—the late president was my father. And yes, my mother and he had a collaboration, but not a sexual one. I learned it was meant to protect me…"

The audience trembled as if struck by lightning. There was noise and shuffling of feet everywhere. The elders of the church could only stare in shock. Elder Mullen approached Monde and quietly whispered, "Ma'am, your speech could harm the ministry."

Monde did not respond but gently assured him with a pat on his right shoulder, signaling that everything would be fine. He retreated.

"Mother, too, had hidden a secret…" Monde continued, "…and that secret is that she had another child. That child is now the head of the Arrogance Cartel. Yes…she had a son with The Boss himself…"

People looked at each other as if an earthquake had struck. News began to spread even before she finished her speech. *Diamond TV, Movie TV*, and *Abantu Bonse Online Media* all reported that the "Veep has taken on her mother and the Arrogance

Cartel" or similar headlines. Some people, especially from the Evangelical communities, began to leave the auditorium.

Monde stepped away from the mic and continued:

"And I...I myself married that man, the new boss of the Arrogance Cartel. His name is Mwanga Bwembya. I met him at Kabulonga High School when he was called Boss Boy. Our relationship started as antagonism and turned into romance... I may, time permitting, explain how the affair blossomed in another forum..."

To the amazement of many, a group of people stood and cheered Monde on, "Go on, Sister, God has finally answered our prayers. We had suspicions but never a chance..."

Meanwhile, Mwanga was fuming in the booth.

"Let's go, Junior..."

"No, Dad, let's hear everything. Look, Mommy is speaking again…"

Mwanga had no choice but to stay.

Besides, if he left at that time, he would be in danger, and the media would descend upon him like a swarm of bees.

All the media houses, except those owned by the government, suspended their programs and switched to live broadcasting.

"Mwanga and I married in a private ceremony at the Intercontinental Hotel…and our wedding took place on the same day my mother died in a plane explosion…"

Monde paused and began to sob. Everyone in the front row wanted to offer her their handkerchiefs, but Gertrude was quicker to wipe her madam's cheeks, and Monde continued.

"…the media reported that only three or five people died that day. But that's not what happened. Since some of the information remains classified, I will reveal what I am privy to. My father-in-law also died that day. Yes, The Boss is dead..."

It was a bombshell.

Television stations stopped all their programming and broadcasted the news.

BREAKING NEWS –

"'The Boss is no more...' Veep Monde, the youngest-ever vice-president in the world, has revealed that The Boss died in the same plane crash that took her mother, Bishop Mwendashi, and President Zeibous..."

The audience received the news with mixed feelings. Those who disliked the drug kingpin began to ululate, dance, and shout for joy. Others who thought that The Boss died a long time ago, were bamboozled by the new.

However, those listening attentively began to question why the president, the bishop, and a kingpin would be on the same plane.

"May I continue…" Monde waved and beckoned to the audience. It calmed down.

"As I was saying, The Boss is dead. And the one who planted the bomb was Jason Mundiyah, the man you all knew as the president's Chief of Staff and political adviser. I truly don't know if this information is classified too, but I have taken a risk here…"

People stood up and shouted, "Say it, Madam Vice-President. The nation has been waiting for a hero, and we have one in you…"

Mwanga sensed that his wife had created a perfect opportunity for an assassination. He instructed all members of the Fraternity to encircle the perimeters of the Grand Cathedral. The Chief of Police in Lusaka, who was also on the payroll of the Arrogance Cartel, was commanded to deploy all uniformed police officers in Lusaka to block all the roads leading to the cathedral.

"General Mushinge, deploy the Zambia Army and Zambia Air Force to provide protection to the Vice-President at the Grand Cathedral."

"As ordered, Mr. President," the joint chief of the army and air force replied.

Gertrude approached Monde and whispered in her ear, "I have received intel that the president is with you...and...you have national protection..."

"My assistant has just assured me that the president is with me and that my safety is assured. Thank you, Mr. President..." Monde said, looking straight into the cameras.

"Now, as I said, and...by the way, when I stepped onto this podium today, I was willing to die, and I still am...I just believe that the truth does not only set people free but also sets nations free..."

When Monde said that, even the skeptical Born-Again diehards stood up and gave a standing ovation. Monde was turning into a national hero. Women, men, and children watching her began to cry, shedding tears of joy. People's hairs stood on end, and it was turning into a revolution. People came and stood at the edge of the cathedral boundary with placards and banners reading, "God has heard us," "Monde, our hero," "She single-handedly is preserving the Christian nation," and many other slogans and mantras.

"...Then, I learned later, when it was already too late, that Mwanga was my half-brother...at this time I was already three months pregnant..."

The audience began to murmur, and the commotion grew louder. The clergy spoke of incest, while non-Christians pontificated the hypocrisy of the Evangelicals and Pentecostals. The audience was split between those who continued to see Monde as a heroine and those beginning to criticize her stance.

"Hear me out first. I would only ask you to bear with me for a few minutes... and then you can lynch me, arrest me, or kill me...I will be all yours..."

Elder Mullen stood up and pleaded with the audience to listen, "...until the end."

Thank you, Gracious Elder, and thank you all for understanding. As I was saying, it was Jason, the president's own political advisor, who killed the president, my mother, and The Boss. I understand that the bomb was initially intended for me and my mother. The president and The Boss were killed by accident. The three were trying to mend relations. In fact, let me disclose it to you all. The president was confronted by The Boss at a recent meeting in Mumbwa with evidence. And he decided to come clean to the nation. I have a video to show in due course. The president was confronted by The Boss about his murders...

The audience erupted in shouts of, "Which murders, whom did he kill..."

There was commotion not only inside the cathedral but also outside through the huge television screens mounted because there was no longer any room inside. People had already gathered at the cathedral before the police and secret services had made barricades around the compound perimeters.

But the shouts of "Let our heroine, our savior, continue..." prevailed, and Monde returned to the podium.

"Again, as I was saying, it was President Zeibous who ordered the arsonist who burned over 630 people to death at the Mulungushi musical festival. That case..."

The people tried to stand and shout "Murderer president, murderer president..." but Monde waved to continue. They gave her the chance.

He also killed General Zebulun Kaichefya, the late and former Army General who was initially the head of the task force assigned to investigate the deadly arson.

The ZIS agent, John Daka, was also killed by President Zeibous.

The president was going to hand himself over to the police and serve any sentence that was adequate or proportional to the crimes he committed.

Recently, I learned that the deal to have President Kaitano Chanda take over as president was arranged because The Boss had convinced President Zeibous that it was the right thing to do. President Zeibous, my father, left me a will, and in it, he admitted to all his crimes.

But the will was not actually left to me; I was only named as the administrator on behalf of the nation. Perhaps he knew that he would be dying or not, I don't know. But he was very clear that all his estates would go to the poor of Zambia.

In due course, I will be discussing this will with the appropriate departments of government...

People stood up and waved anything they held in their hands—Bibles, shoes, scarves, pieces of paper, hats—chanting, "Long live Monde, our savior. Long live fearless corruption buster!"

The room was literally shaking. But as the room shook, some people in strategic places began to sense danger. Groups started to protest across the nation. Rallies began popping up in all ten provinces of Zambia.

"And like you, I was a victim of the bridled public perception that turned The Boss into this mafioso kingpin who hated the country and saturated it with illegal substances until I met the man and his work. You and I can even find ourselves inadequate before this tower of a man..."

After saying that, the audience became riled with indignation. They demanded an explanation of why a criminal and drug lord could be justified, if at all. One person shouted, "The devil is still a devil even if he wears Prada."

...indeed, I agree with that gentleman's sentiment, except, I beg you to hear me out, and then judge how reasonable or unreasonable my words may be.

We boast of the only aircraft liner in the nation, the Zamair—he owned it.

The only scientific laboratory in the country, the Shichakufwaya Research Institute in Kabwe—he owned it.

The Mutivera Pharmaceuticals, the only medicinal company that manufactures painkillers and antibiotics in Zambia—he owned it.

The now largely international airport in Zambia, the Nchanga International Airport in Chingola—he owned it.

He owned the largest share in our copper mines—yes, he owned it.

The now largest university with the best facilities and conditions of service for its employees, Mutandis University—he…

"…owns it…" the audience chanted.

"The Melekiah, the Frontline, and the Levy Junction malls in Zambia, he…"

"…bought and owned them…"

"The fastest overland train system in Africa, the Nyanji Transit Corporation, famously known as the NTC, he…"

"…owns it…"

"The…"

The chants became sustained and all one could hear was the phrase "owns it" or "owned it" echoing throughout the auditorium and across the nation.

When the chants had subsided, Monde paused momentarily and then said, "He has more assets than the government, he employs more people than the government, and he has put Zambia on the map better than the Zambian government…"

The people in the audience and across the nation began to beat their chests. "He pays and feeds my family every year," one man declared.

"He provides me with contracts for my cotton farming," a woman shouted.

Then a wave of attestations followed, with people associating themselves with his companies or products directly or indirectly. Monde sobbed for a few seconds before dropping another bombshell.

"You know," she began, "…he was incarcerated in prison, and my father went on to win a second term as president. The entire nation thought my father was the hero. But do you know that he owned the company that provided security and the one that performed maintenance for all the prisons in Zambia?"

That revelation silenced even the diehard skeptics in the audience. At that moment, everyone became a believer. The man the nation had hated with fear and trembling became, in the blink of an eye, the most beloved figure in the nation.

When that revelation hit the streets, a revolution was underway. People began to demand that The Boss be offered unconditional amnesty. Government offices were flooded with people even as late as midnight. Streets were inundated with honking cars waving Zambian flags, singing, "The Boss must return," organically.

Then Monde said, "Fortunately, The Boss' body remains in state, embalmed somewhere on a farm... and on behalf of my husband, I ask that he be granted a state funeral."

The crowd's reaction showed that the people were pleased with the request.

As the *Monde Allegations* piled up, the president called for a joint session with his Cabinet and all opposition leaders in

Zambia. They met at 2:00 am in the situation room at State House. The first resolution they made that morning, Monde later learned, was to drop all the charges and criminal convictions against The Boss posthumously and bestow upon him the Order of Zambia medal, also posthumously.

They declared him a national treasure and conferred upon him a state funeral. Monde also learned that they acquiesced to her request to set up a truce and reconciliation commission (the "Commission") and appointed Monde, in absentia, as the commissioner of the Commission. However, the president rejected Monde's request to resign as vice-president.

"September the first will henceforth be known as *Monde Mwendashi Day*, the day Zambia came to grips with its destiny," President Chanda declared.

Everyone present nodded in agreement. Some members excused themselves and left, but most of the Cabinet members remained in the situation room.

Even as Monde continued to speak, President Chanda looked at his iPhone. The Arrogance Cartel had unleashed videos incriminating as many people in his circles as he knew, including the opposition leaders and himself. The videos ranged from corruption to bribery to sexual harassment to possession of illegal real estate properties.

The president's world was collapsing. Then a message appeared, reading, "These are for your information only; Arrogance Cartel and the vice-president will not disclose them to anyone." Then the message and the video disappeared from his phone.

"Was I dreaming?" The president rubbed his eyes repeatedly. Once his vision cleared, he looked at the television, and Monde was still speaking.

> Now, I want to end with what is very close to my heart. My husband and I came to an agreement, and the Arrogance Cartel or AC is considering it.
>
> All of the AC's assets will be returned to the people.

CHARLES MWEWA

> The only thing they are asking is to create a truce and reconciliation commission, which I will chair.
>
> The government must declare an amnesty for all members of the AC, past and present, so that they are not prosecuted.
>
> Once the commission is formed, I will resign from both my positions as leader of Grand Cathedral Church and as Vice-President…

Monde had barely finished speaking before she was whisked away. Secret Service agents on duty had received intelligence that it had become a clear and present danger moment for the vice-president. A helicopter was already waiting for her on the roof of the cathedral.

Back at the library, the *Monde Allegations*, as they became known in Zambia, were the main subject of discussion. Many of the AC members had never known a life of freedom. They were born into danger and grew up surrounded by it. Monde was introducing a new paradigm. They were potentially gazing at freedom itself if the truce and reconciliation commission completed its mission favorably.

"The first thing I will do if the Commission succeeds is to try and locate my twin brother," said one woman who had been separated from her twin brother when they were barely seven years old.

"As for me," Dr. Phiri Sr. retorted, "I want to drive my Bentley freely along Cairo Road."

"And you, Boss?" Shokashoka asked.

"I want to visit LFC and munch the fast food very slowly," he joked.

Just as they were having fun, a phone rang. It was from the truce and reconciliation commission chairperson.

"Hello, it's me, your wife, but…"

"In your capacity as the chair, I know…"

"Yes, what do you expect to hear on…"

"My especially complicated position… right?"

"Yes, Darling. There is good news and bad news. What do you want to hear first?"

"Give me the good news first…"

"Sure, the bad news is that the commission feels that to placate society, you and Shokashoka should serve at least house arrest and some community service for seven months before…"

"We are completely freed… I understand. I can agree to that. And what's the good news?"

"That you will keep all the haciendas…"

"You mean all seventeen of them?"

"I mean it, including all that they are not aware of… but…"

"You said it was good news, so why the buts?"

"It's still good news, but they want full disclosure of all assets in foreign accounts."

"Sure, I will provide that. Tell them I will comply."

"Okay, there will be a public ceremony to seal the deal. Are you comfortable?"

"Well, we are moving from darkness into the light. Why wouldn't I? I want to be honest before men and God…"

"I have all that I needed to know. Bye, Darling…"

"See you later…"

The phone had been ringing. He had worked until 3:00 a.m. that day without resting. He was exhausted by the time he pressed the "send" button on his HP laptop computer.

"Y-yes, wha-t's going on?"

The Team, with the exception of Matafwali, was on the group call on WhatsApp.

"We're all here—me, Katuta, Dorothy, and Nalu…"

"All right, what's the deal?"

"What's the deal, what's the deal? You are the deal," Katuta bragged.

"Morgie, you rocked, man. You've turned the nation upside down," Nalumino disclosed.

It had been a tough decision for Mwanga. Hitting that button might render the nation ungovernable, he understood. But he also knew that the problem of corruption had reached endemic levels, and delaying would only exacerbate the situation.

I must inform... I must... tell it all, and by telling the truth, can we be free, he thought.

Then he had called the Team and advised them of his decision.

"What did you decide, Sir?" Dorothy had asked.

"Tell us, Sir," Katuta begged.

"Is it a 'no,' Sir?" Nalumino predicted.

"I am going for 'yes,' Team. I slept over it, and I have a clear conscience that it is the right thing to do. And... I have asked Morgan to go ahead and release the stash," Mwanga declared.

The command was given around 5:00 p.m. But it took Morgan over ten hours to reorganize materials worth twenty years of collection on just about everyone who mattered in the country.

He started with information on older forms of gadgets.

These diskettes are dusty, but they are still in good condition, he thought.

Then he downloaded and sorted all the files. What he saw made him realize that one of the most significant reasons for the nation's lack of development was corruption. He continued to think, "I am now sure of it."

He discovered university lecturers and professors selling exam questions to students; students sneaking into college and school vaults to steal exam materials;

government ministers accepting kickbacks; company executives paying hush money to silence sexual assault claims; ruling and opposition politicians buying votes; city councilors manipulating rules to redistribute land and public market plots; and church clergy engaging in inappropriate behavior with young girls and boys.

"Oh, my God!" Morgan shouted, speaking to himself in shock.

He found that airport authorities, court officials and judges, municipal workers, civil servants, licensing departments, and many others were deeply corrupt.

What kind of nation can this be at this rate? he thought.

Then he accessed more recent technologies, such as cloud-based storage, and opened multiple files. Morgan almost fell off his seat.

The former president's sponsored murders, corruption involving chiefs of the army, the police, anti-corruption commission, anti-drug and money-laundering commissions, air force, and government officials were all captured.

Who is normal in this country? Morgan thought, "The Boss is right. It's time to purge the nation."

Then Morgan pressed the "send" button and went to sleep.

When he was woken up by the Team around 9:00 a.m. that morning, he did not know what impact the release of the incriminating information would have on the nation.

"Morgie, there's pandemonium, dude, in a good way for the innocent, of course," Dorothy informed.

"The nation is in a state of—no, not emergency—of panic. No, protests! Yes, protests like you've never seen before," Katuta was emphatic.

"The president is almost declaring martial law; the army is on standby, according to Madam Vice-President," Nalumino notified.

As they were talking on the phone, Katuta shared a video with the group of what had just happened around Manda Hill, the country's parliament building.

"Kevin Hambolelwa, the Speaker, has just been mugged by the mob because of the video you posted, Morgie, which showed him being bribed by the opposition in the adoption of the Same-Sex Bill, which, of course, failed to become law," Katuta explained.

Then Dorothy jumped in and read:

> Look at this. The *National Mirror* has just published a story based on the video you posted, Morgie, of Susane Katongo who confirmed that the image in the video is her and Chief Justice Morris Katema. She was paid hush money to remain silent. She produced a check signed by the clerk of the Supreme Court for an undisclosed amount. The amount was redacted.

As the Team continued to receive breaking news throughout that morning, it became clear that Zambia was facing an

unprecedented moment since
independence.

***

"No, Mr. President, I am against the idea of
declaring a state of martial law. I will go out
there and address the nation on your
behalf. You see, even your credibility is
affected… you appear in one of those
videos receiving a payment from an Anglo-
American company in the cobalt deal…"

"I am aware of that… and I'll own up to
my mistake, although I had returned it…
but you're right, martial law will be
construed as me trying to hide that reality."

"And… Mr. President, are you going to
reshuffle this government? I need to
mention that in my address…"

"Yes, thank God for you, Ma'am,
otherwise, there would be no credibility left
in this administration…"

"Of course, we are in this together…
Besides, the cobalt deal never went through
anyway… but three-quarters of your

ministers received bribes, and the information is out there in the public square…"

"It's a shame, I feel…"

Before the president could complete his sentence, a reporter from ZNBC was already in the situation room, ready to set up the vice-president for a national address.

"Are you ready, Madam Vice-President?"

"Yes, Melinda, let's do this…"

Melinda Broom worked on the final touches with her technical staff, ensuring everything was ready for the national address of State House.

"Countrymen and women," Monde began.

"As the wheel of change beckons, I come to you with the president's message. The president is not resigning, as that would make our nation ungovernable. Rather, the president promises the nation that he is reshuffling his Cabinet with immediate effect. Within 120 days, there will be elections to choose a new president and MPs.

"I urge for calm, because your voice has been heard. As the one who started this battle, I appeal to you all to return to your homes. This will give us the time to review all that has been disclosed by AC. I promise you that we will return this country to sanity, and that will be very soon…"

As the vice-president addressed the nation, State House staff began reporting to the president that calm had returned. People had heard the vice-president's address and believed her.

"She has our best interests at heart, and she is right there at State House, so we are giving the government the benefit of the doubt," one woman posted on her *Telegraph* social media profile. Many people on *Facebook*, *X*, and *TikTok* held a similar view.

Monde had done it again. But the calmness would prove to be momentary as more people were just waking up to view the dumped videos.

[17] THE AFTERMATH

Monde and Mwanga, flanked by a retinue including Mary Munthali, Benjamin Kalasa, Henry Phiri, Gertrude Shinde, Matafwali Kalonji, and young Bwembya Mwendashi, attended the launch of a mausoleum recently built to house the remains of The Boss. Designed by a Chinese engineer selected from among 50 architectural firms, the mausoleum had an elaborate oriental feel but epitomized modernity, especially on the inside. It was described by the *Times of Zambia* as a temple befitting a "benevolent kingpin with a heart of gold."

Mwanga had appointed Benjamin Kalasa to deliver the eulogy.

My friend and brother, you finally rest in a gorgeous temple at the heart of the city, after spending your life in hiding. You faced all kinds of dangers, arrests, impeachments, disappointments, betrayals, and even castration, with a clear conscience, just to bring this land into a new dawn.

Your methods were unorthodox and even criminal, yet at the core, you loved all and believed in all.

In your will, you bequeathed the People's Enterprise Ltd. to the young people of Zambia, and I am delighted to report that your son has appointed me as the director in charge.

I want you to know that I will live up to your expectations and principles. I will ensure that no child lacks a quality education, no boy or girl roams the streets without shelter, and no little one perishes from curable diseases.

You, my friend, have left us with a cushion to lay our heads on—your son, our new leader. He has given all *Assistanzas* back to their families with exceptional retirement pecks.

You should have been here to see how, together with his wife, the capable and incorruptible Vice President of the nation, they have changed the economic and political outlooks of Zambia, respectively.

Because of them, and indeed because of you, Zambia was recently reclassified as a semi-developed country, trending towards zero corruption.

I am happy to be alive to report all these achievements to you, and I look forward to joining you where you are.

I have been reassured that I will be rested here when my time comes, continuing to honor your legacy, and to serve you in world of the dead…

No one even noticed when Benjamin finished his eulogy.

People were crying inconsolably. Children and the elderly paraded through the streets to walk past the mausoleum. Major local, regional, and international news outlets reported on the man and his resting place.

"May I speak?" interrupted a hoarse voice from the crowd.

"My name is Kelvin Savimbi, famously known as 'Bones.'"

As soon as he mentioned "Bones," all the major reporters turned their attention toward him. He was also known as "The Wind" because, despite the Angola government's efforts, including with the help of the CIA, no one knew his whereabouts. He was deemed the "richest man alive in Africa" and he was a drug lord.

"I have been deeply touched by what my old friend, who rests here, has done for Zambia. I'm giving all my wealth to the people of Angola," he declared, inviting Interpol to arrest him on the spot.

The crowd erupted with chants of "Even in death the Boss remains an influencer," and people shouted with joy.

Massive headlines across the globe reported how a drug kingpin's death had brought blessings to a nation and helped to end corruption.

Mwanga and Monde glanced at each other and smiled.

"The *PLAN* became a reality," Mwanga began.

"Indeed, it did, by the grace of God," Monde completed.

***

"Look, Darling, I found something in the Bible: 'The nakedness of your sister, the daughter of your father, or the daughter of your mother, whether born at home or elsewhere, their nakedness you shall not uncover.'"

"So, what about it, Mr. Bwembya?" Monde teased.

"That was from Leviticus 18:9. I also read Genesis 20:12: 'Indeed, she is truly my sister. She is the daughter of my father, but not the daughter of my mother; and she became my wife.'"

"What are you getting at, a guilty conscience, hmm?"

"I started feeling a bit guilty, but I think I want to make another baby with you. You know, it's been a while…"

"Oh, silly… I prayed for it. I think I'm alright with *our* marriage; it'd be a greater sin to divorce when we married in ignorance. After all…"

"After all what?"

"We're not from the same father and mother…"

Before Monde could finish her sentence, Mwanga was all over her.

"Be gentle, silly, I haven't done *it* in seven years…"

"Oh… oh…" Mwanga was already to the third heavens and back.

As they lay there, as plain as they came from their mothers' wombs, they began to reflect on past events and where they were.

"How is the *Animal Man* doing?" Monde asked.

"He's still going through rehab… you know, we pulled quite a trick on him…"

"What about the redistribution project?"

"On that one, I've accomplished almost ninety-nine percent. You already read in today's papers that Zambia's poverty data has shocked the rest of the world. We injected about US$260 billion back into the Zambian economy. If we continue at this pace, we could become the fastest country on the path to becoming the first developed nation in Africa..."

"Really, *Boss Boy*..."

"Don't call me that, I'm *redeemed*, or..."

"Or what... *it* is getting up again... no... not again, I am not a procreation machine..."

"Who said that you're *not*..."

***

THE *MAST* EDITORIAL –

"'Could it have been done better...?'

Only history will show how one

young woman, or probably two young people, changed a nation. It's as it was captured in the editorial of last week under the heading, 'How the mighty have fallen…' Indeed, corruption, the biggest menace to this nation, has been dethrone by a simply at of honesty and bravery. Monde put everything on the line – her inheritance, Veep position, head of the grandest church in Zambia, and even her own safety – to bring the beast out of its hideout and then single-handedly to murder it in front of the entire nation.

We will never know how this story end, but what is clear and true, is that Zambia is on its way to a genuine recovery, to what Mwanga himself described as, "The truth that set us all free.

"The Mast *is discussing your successes, Darling*," Mwanga whispered into his wife's right here.

"*It's yours, too, but more of the* people's," Monde whispered back.

The couple nodded with their heads and fell asleep.

[EPILOGUE]

The story of Zambia was not over, at least not yet. Deep roots of corruption and murders ran through the nation's political and economic terrain.

The *Monde Allegations* had brought the nation to the brink of a revolution. It was a "soft revolution" as one commentator put it. But it had the potential to order a reset.

A disbanded drug cartel held the key to the revelations in which it was also complicit. But the price of liberty knew no sacrifice Zambians could not brace.

Whether it took a mistake of nature or a

marriage of convenience, or, indeed, the route through purgatory itself, the sanity of the nation had to be salvaged at all costs or perish trying to salvage it.

www.ingramcontent.com/pod-product-compliance
Lightning Source LLC
Chambersburg PA
CBHW071625270326
41928CB00010B/1786